Autoethnography as Feminist Method

Autoethnography is an ideal method to study the 'feminist I'. Through personal stories, the author reflects on how feminists negotiate agency and the effect this has on one's political sensibilities. Speaking about oneself transforms into stories of political responsibility – a key issue for feminists who function as cultural mediators.

Professor Elizabeth Ettorre is an internationally known feminist sociologist. She has written in the areas of substance misuse, genetics, reproduction and autoethnography. Currently, she is Emerita Professor of Sociology, University of Liverpool, UK; Honorary Professor, Aarhuus University, Denmark and University of Plymouth, UK; and Docent in Sociology, University of Helsinki, Finland and Åbo Akademi University, Finland.

Autoethnography as Feminist Method

Sensitising the feminist 'I'

Elizabeth Ettorre

LONDON AND NEW YORK

First published 2017
by Routledge

2 Park Square, Milton Park, Abingdon, Oxfordshire OX14 4RN
52 Vanderbilt Avenue, New York, NY 10017

Routledge is an imprint of the Taylor & Francis Group, an informa business

First issued in paperback 2019

Copyright © 2017 Elizabeth Ettorre

The right of Elizabeth Ettorre to be identified as author of this work has been asserted by her in accordance with sections 77 and 78 of the Copyright, Designs and Patents Act 1988.

All rights reserved. No part of this book may be reprinted or reproduced or utilised in any form or by any electronic, mechanical, or other means, now known or hereafter invented, including photocopying and recording, or in any information storage or retrieval system, without permission in writing from the publishers.

Notice:
Product or corporate names may be trademarks or registered trademarks, and are used only for identification and explanation without intent to infringe.

British Library Cataloguing in Publication Data
A catalogue record for this book is available from the British Library

Library of Congress Cataloging in Publication Data
A catalog record for this book has been requested

ISBN: 978-1-138-64788-6 (hbk)
ISBN: 978-0-367-87732-3 (pbk)

Typeset in Times New Roman
by Sunrise Setting Ltd., Brixham, UK

To my precious friend and partner, Imma, with whom I am blessed to share my life

Contents

About the author		viii
Preface		ix
Acknowledgements		xi
Introduction: autoethnography as feminist method		1
1	Being a 'sexual pervert' in academia	24
2	Finding my feminist voice through an illness story: 'An old female body confronts a thyroid problem'	43
3	Doing feminist autoethnography with drug-using women	60
4	*'She wrote it but look what she wrote'*	74
5	Sensitizing the feminist 'I'	99
Index		120

About the author

Elizabeth Ettorre is an internationally known feminist sociologist in the area of substance misuse, genetics, reproduction and autoethnography. She is Emerita Professor of Sociology, University of Liverpool, UK; Honorary Professor, Aarhuus University, Denmark and University of Liverpool, UK; and Docent in Sociology, University of Helsinki, Finland and Åbo Akademi University, Finland. As well as publishing in a number of international journals, her scholarly books include *Gendering Addiction: The Politics of Drug Treatment in a Neurochemical World* (with N. Campbell); *Culture, Bodies and the Sociology of Health*; *Revisioning Women and Drug Use: Gender, Power and the Body*; *Making Lesbians Visible in the Substance Use Field*; *Reproductive Genetics, Gender and the Body*; *Before Birth: Understanding Prenatal Screening*; *Women and Alcohol: From a Private Pleasure to a Public Problem?*; *Society, the Body and Well-Being* (with K. Suolinna and E. Lahelma); *Gendered Moods: Psychotropics and Society* (with Elianne Riska); *Women and Substance Use*; *Drug Services in England and the Impact of the Central Funding Initiative* (with S. MacGregor, R. Coomber and A. Crosier) and *Lesbians, Women and Society*.

Preface

I am very happy to write *Autoethnography as Feminist Method: Sensitising the feminist 'I'*. I am aware after forty years in academia, I still have something important and hopefully thought-provoking to say. I wrote this book as a way of sharing with my readers one of the most intellectually stimulating and just plain enjoyable experiences I have had in my whole academic life: a four-month Leverhulme Emeritus Fellowship, 'Writing the self, the other and the social: using autoethnography as a feminist method of 'sensitising the I', which I was awarded from December 2014 to March 2015. During that time I visited a number of feminists[1] and feminist oriented research centres in the US, UK, Sweden and Finland. I think it is very interesting that I had this experience as a retired, feminist professor of sociology. It says something about the nature of academia and how it treats women[2] that I had to wait until I am retired to achieve such satisfaction. Of course, I am aware that this is probably not true for everyone, but it still demonstrates that in a career spanning over forty years since the late 1970s, I have had to wait until retirement to experience such a high point of intellectual stimulation.

Autoethnography as Feminist Method: Sensitising the feminist 'I' draws on conversations from my discussions[3] with feminists and other colleagues, including a number of bright postgraduate students at various institutions that I visited, as well as my personal diaries including records of key events with dates, places, people, feelings, emotions and bodily states during my fellowship time. Although I am aware that feminists have been doing autoethnographic work (see, for example, Holman-Jones, 2005 and Ellis 1995) there has not yet been a book project that focuses on autoethnography as feminist method. I want to show how using the feminist 'I' is an important contribution to contemporary feminisms' 'writing the self' and autoethnography as an intimate account of being feminist in today's society.

Elizabeth Ettorre
Lapland, Finland
April 2016

Notes

1 For me, using the term 'feminist' includes a 'broad church' so to speak; in other words, not only 'women'.

2 For a contemporary view of what it is like to be a woman in academia, see http://www.slate.com/blogs/quora/2016/01/28/what_are_challenges_faced_by_women_in_academia.html?wpsrc=sh_all_dt_em_bot (accessed 19 February 2016).
3 During my Leverhulme Fellowship, I had about 30 hours of discussions with a number of colleagues about autoethnography, of which 11.5 hours were digitally recorded and transcribed by myself.

References

Ellis, C. (1995) *Final Negotiations: A Story of Love, Loss and Chronic Illness*. Philadelphia, PA: Temple University Press.

Holman-Jones, S. (2005) 'Autoethnography: making the personal political'. In Denzin, N. K. and Lincoln, Y. S. (eds.), *The Sage Handbook of Qualitative Research*. 3rd edn. Thousand Oaks, CA: Sage Publications, pp. 763–91.

Acknowledgements

This book is the result of a four-month Leverhulme Emeritus Fellowship, *'Writing the self, the other and the social: using autoethnography as a feminist method of "sensitising the I"'*, which I was awarded from December 2014 to March 2015 by The Leverhulme Trust, London, UK. I thank the Trust for this wonderful opportunity. I am particularly grateful to Anna Grundy, Grants Manager at the Trust for her helpful advice during the duration of my award.

There were a number of people who helped to make my Fellowship a success. They are colleagues and friends at various academic institutions. They all deserve a special thanks for their warmth, hospitality, support and friendship. They include Dr Kirsti Lempianen, University of Lapland, Rovaniemi, Finland; Professors Margrit Shildrick and Nina Lykke, University of Linköping, Sweden; Professor Steven Miles, Manchester Metropolitan University, UK; Professor Gayle Letherby, Carol Sutton, University of Plymouth, UK; Professor Barbara Katz Rothman, City University of New York, NY, US; Professor Nancy Campbell, Rensselaer Polytechnic Institute, Troy, NY, US and last, but not least, Professors Carolyn Ellis, Arthur Bochner and Dr Sara Crawley, University of South Florida, FL, US. There were a number of colleagues and students I met at these universities during my Leverhulme travels. I would like to thank them all for inspiring me and sharing their ideas with me.

I would also like to thank:

- Tim and Theresa McGowan, Drorah Setel, Rochester, NY, US; my sister, Barbara Ettorre, and my brother, James Ettorre and his partner Mary Olson, New York, NY, US; Frankie Sandra Crookes, Newton, CT, US. They all offered me warmth and hospitality during my research visit Stateside.
- Sage Publications for giving me permission to publish part of my previously published 2010 article, 'Nuns, dykes, drugs and gendered bodies: an autoethnography of a lesbian feminist's journey through "good time" sociology" (originally in *Sexualities* 13, 3: 295–315) in Chapter 1 of this book. I also thank Ken Plummer, Susanne MacGregor, Barbara Katz Rothman, Carol Smart, Jeany Elston, Irmeli Laitinen, Carol Sutton, Matthew David, Steve Miles, Ciara Kierans and Jude Robinson for encouraging me to publish the article used in the first chapter.

xii *Acknowledgements*

- Elsevier for giving me permission to publish part of my previously published 2005 article 'Gender, older female bodies and autoethnography: finding my feminist voice by telling my illness story' (originally in *Women's Studies International Forum* 28: 535–46) in Chapter 2 of the book. I am very grateful to Barbara Katz Rothman, Gillian Hundt, Jeany Elson, Malcolm Williams for their helpful comments on an earlier version of this published paper.
- Taylor & Francis for giving me permission to publish part of my previously published 2013 article 'Drug user researchers as autoethnographers: "doing reflexivity" with women drug users' (originally in *Substance Use & Misuse* 48: 1377–85) in Chapter 3 of the book. I want to extend a big thank you to the women who shared their stories with me, 'Kitty' for introducing them to me, Dr Lyvinia Elleschild for transcribing these conversations and for translating some of the local drug 'argot' and Dr Irmeli Laitinen for giving very helpful comments on the first draft of the published paper.
- Gerhard Boomgaarden, Senior Publisher at Routledge for commissioning this book, his encouragement and just plain friendliness, and also Alyson Claffey, Senior Editorial Assistant in Sociology at Routledge for her help in the final stages of publishing this book.

There are a number of friends and colleagues who gave support, advice and encouragement before and during the writing process. They include Dr Matthew David, University of Durham, UK; Dr Liz Davidson, Liverpool, UK; Professor Cindy Fazey, University of Liverpool, UK; Professor Rosanna Hertz, Wellesley College, MA, US; Professor Geoffrey Hunt, Aarhuus University, Denmark and Institute for Scientific Analysis, Alameda, CA, US; Dr Irmeli Laitinen, Helsinki, Finland; Professor Susanne MacGregor, London School of Hygiene and Tropical Medicine, UK; Dr Maggie Ornstein, Sarah Lawrence College, Bronxville, NY, US; Dr Maya Maor, Ben Gurion University of the Negrev, Israel; Professor Nancy Naples, University of Connecticut, CT, US and Professor Deborah Steinberg, University of Warwick, UK.

I should also like to thank Andee Rudolff, a consultant and artist working predominantly in Kentucky and Tennessee, US, who has been consistently generous to me by allowing me to use her wonderful art work on my book covers, including this one (see http://www.chicnhair.com/).

Introduction
Autoethnography as feminist method

Being a feminist fieldworker means that I attend to the subtleties of inequalities (in race, class, gender, sexual orientation, ability, age, etc.), including the ways in which I live out sexist programming.

(Kleinman, 2003: 230)

Feminism and autoethnograpy

In this introductory chapter, I place autoethnography firmly within the tradition of feminist narrative writing and the literary turn within ethnography. I see autoethnography as just one way of doing feminism in society and, as many of us are aware, there are many ways of doing feminism. When I first started to look at autoethnography as a feminist method, I became increasingly mindful that disenchantment with the dominant Cartesian paradigm of rationality at the heart of modern social sciences led us as scholars to narrative. We did this because narrative emphasizes plurality of truths that all cultures claim about themselves. Narrative shifts or pushes us from notions that there is a single cultural perspective revealing an irrefutable set of truths; and through narrative, any scholar can achieve an understanding of personal experiences 'beyond specific historical contexts or shifting relations of power and inequalities' (Bell, 2000: 139). For me, narrative methods generate useful ways of creating knowledge about individuals, collective agency and the interior language of emotional vulnerability and at times, wounding, which to me is at the heart of good autoethnography.

In this context, I want to discuss Hannah Arendt's impact on narrative, which I see as relevant to this discussion. Benhabib (1990: 187–8), researching Arendt's relationship to narrative, discusses narrative or storytelling as 'a fundamental human activity', while contending that 'the narrative structure of action . . . determines the identity of the self'.[1] In her work, Hannah Arendt (1998: 184) tells us that 'stories (or narratives) are living realities' and it is through 'action and speech that we insert ourselves in the world'. For her, we are 'not the authors or producers' of our own life stories, but rather there are many 'actors, speakers and sufferers' who exist in the 'web of human relationships' wherever men (*sic*) live together – but 'no authors' (1998: 184). This is because stories (i.e. narratives) 'pre-exist every individual, set the context for their activities, and shape the way actors are understood, responded to and remembered' (Bowring, 2013: 18). I mentioned Arendt's work because the fact that she understood her political theorising as storytelling is instructive to autoethnographers who, as storytellers, perceive the theorising of our stories as political. Simply, on the one hand, with Arendt we see the redemptive power of narrative (Benhabib, 1990). On the other hand, with autoethnography, we see the transformative power of 'writing the self', transforming personal stories into political realities by revealing power inequalities inherent in human relationships and the complex cultures of emotions embedded in these unequal relationships.

Narrative 'writing the self' has been recognised as an important method for feminists for a number of years (Stanley, 1992, 1993, 1994), while interest in feminist autobiography has grown (Cosslett et al., 2000; Maynes et al., 2008; Smart, 2007). Autoethnography can be seen as a form of autobiographical writing, but, I would argue, autoethnography is very different from autobiography. I would like to take a slight diversion here. In my experience, colleagues who do not practice autoethnography or are not autoethnographers themselves often tend to place autoethnography within the field of autobiography, memoire, etc. Some scholars go so far as to conclude that there is no difference between autobiography and autoethnography or that the difference between them is minimal. During my Leverhulme Emeritus Fellowship and after a plethora of discussions with colleagues, I am able to differentiate clearly between autoethnography and autobiography. Autobiographical research is mainly concerned with placing the 'I' within a personal context and developing insights from that perspective. It may be political or it may not. On the other hand, autoethnography, although 'an autobiographical genre of writing and research',[2] is all about placing the 'I' firmly within a cultural context and all that that implies. However, there is one clear similarity between feminist autobiography and feminist autoethnograpy – both share Liz Stanley's (1993: 133)[3] view that the 'self' is enormously 'complex' and 'feminist conceptualising of the self, within as well as across conventional discipline boundaries, needs to be correspondingly complex'.

Although autoethnography is writing the self-reflexive-self (Reed-Danahay, 1997a), autoethnography is all about describing the cultural dynamics that an individual confronts rather than personal dynamics as in traditional autobiography.[4] For me, autoethnography exposes the individual in a matrix of always and already political activities as one passes through one's cultural experiences. Furthermore, in asking the epistemological question 'how do we know what we know?', autoethnographers demonstrate that autoethnography is perhaps more versatile than autobiography because it reveals several levels of consciousness that link the personal to the cultural (Ellis and Bochner, 2000: 739). Simply, knowledge comes from political understandings of one's social positioning as well as experiences of the cultural freedoms and constraints one encounters. Hopefully, this will become clear for the reader in Chapters 1 and 4.

Autoethnography along with the 'I' in the social sciences (Katz Rothman, 2005, 2007) has made a firm incursion into feminism specifically (Averett, 2009; Boylorn, 2013; Griffin, 2012; Shomali, 2012) and narrative methods generally (Ellis, 1995, 2004, 2009; Ellis and Bochner, 1996). For me, I see autoethnography lying definitely within the realm of postmodern (critical theory) ethnography (O'Byrne, 2007), and being a study of culture that involves the self, although it is viewed often as unconventional or narcissistic in relation to established academic canons (Anderson, 2006). Additionally, autoethnography may create problems when trying to navigate the politics of university bureaucracies (Forber-Pratt, 2015).

Defined as 'an autobiographical genre of writing and research that displays multiple layers of consciousness, connecting the personal to the cultural' (Ellis and Bochner, 2000: 739), autoethnography is a reformulation of the traditional binary emic (observed) and etic (observer) positions with emphasis on research process (graphy), culture (ethnos) and self (auto) (Reed-Danahay, 1997b). Writing in the first person, autoethnographers look back and forth 'through an ethnographic wide-angle lens, focusing outward on cultural aspects of personal experience (Chang, 2008); then inward, exposing a vulnerable self' moved by refracting and resisting cultural interpretations (Ellis and Bochner, 2000: 739). In this way, autoethnographers are sceptical of positivistic research, they question 'grand narratives which claim objectivity, authority and researcher neutrality in the study of social and cultural life' and reject 'the assumed ubiquity of stable meanings, existing independently of culture, social context and researcher activity and interpretation' (Short *et al.*, 2013: 3).

Evaluated through the lens of science and art, autoethnography bridges the gap between scientific and literary writing. Important criteria in judging the value of autoethnography include copious detail, temporal structure revolving between past and present, emotional integrity of the author reflecting deeply on one's actions, a plausible journey of transition from 'who I was to who I am', ethical awareness for others and a reader moved by the story (Bochner, 2000: 270).

Adele Clarke (2005: 8–9) contends that autoethnography is part of the postmodernist re-representational interventions which, unlike traditional narrative analysis or 'grounded theory's analytic centering on social phenomenon, such as being raced, gendered or classed, offers a different qualitative approach focusing on individuals or collectivities'. The strength of autoethnography is that not only does it 'successfully represent in another medium – such as oral interview into scholarly writing' (Clarke, 2005: 34) but, as an authentic method, it also locates research experience in the changing ebb of emotional life, allowing interpretations of personal 'truths' and speaking about oneself to transform into narrative representations of political responsibility (Ettorre, 2010) – an important issue for feminists who often function as cultural mediators. Representationally, handling those politics with great care is crucial (Clarke, 2005: 127). Autoethnographers present particular embodied events and emotions with people in time, their social shaping, evolutions and how these events are emblematic of wider cultural meanings and social trends (Neville-Jan, 2004; Sparkes, 2003). Although autoethnography relates to the social scientific tradition, it has no allegiance to any one discipline (Wolcott, 2004). It is truly inter-disciplinary and employed in sociology, anthropology, media studies, literary work, journalism, performance, communication, geography, public health, management studies and perhaps, surprisingly, musicology (see Bartleet and Ellis, 2009).

Autoethnography as feminist method

Allen and Piercy (2005: 156) define feminist autoethnography as 'a method of being, knowing and doing that combines two concerns: telling the stories of those who are marginalized and making good use of our experience'. They also contend that we as feminists no longer 'insist on being dispassionate or positioned outside the hermeneutic circle in order to make valid contributions to knowledge' (2005: 156). Building on Allen and Percy's concerns, I envisage four ways (although these are not complete or exhaustive) in which autoethnography is a feminist method: (1) autoethnography creates transitional, intermediate spaces, inhabiting the crossroads or borderlands of embodied emotions; (2) autoethnography is an active demonstration of the 'personal is political'; (3) autoethnography is feminist critical writing which is performative, that is committed to the future of women and (4) autoethnography helps to raise oppositional consciousness by exposing precarity.

Autoethnography creates transitional, intermediate spaces, inhabiting the crossroads or borderlands of embodied emotions

When feminists do autoethnography we become acutely aware that we are doing a method which allows for the formation of critical, interpretative space. Doing autoethnography, we give way to an intimate, intermediate space, which includes ambiguity, uncertainty and equivocality. In her book, *Anthropology that Breaks Your Heart*, Ruth Behar (1996: 174) talks about what happens when academics challenge methodologically or theoretically the orthodoxies of the academy. She envisages that when we make these challenges we create 'a borderland between passion and intellect, analysis and subjectivity ethnography and autobiography, art and life'. Often quoted, these words were conceived initially in Behar's dialogue with the works of Gloria Anzaldua (1987) in her classic text, *Borderlands, La Frontera: The New Mestiza*. Anzaldua talks about *la mestiza* who walks in one culture and out of another but is in all cultures at the same time (1987: 99). *La mestiza* is in the state of being beyond binary ('either–or') conceptions. *La mestiza* is the state of being 'both' and 'and'. *La mestiza* has a tolerance for ambiguity and contradictions (1987: 101). Inhabiting the crossroads forms the *mesitza* consciousness. *La mestiza* must live without borders and be a cross between an insider and an outsider and she must be herself a crossroads (1987: 217).

As a feminist autoethnographer, I am similar to *la mestiza*. I am an embodied crossroads. As I occupy this *in between space*, I craft a transitional space of understanding between me, myself and the other. Often, the boundaries between us become blurred. Writing in my first-person voice, I learn how to identify the ambiguity of personal and social relationships. It is as if I look through an ethnographic wide-angle lens, focusing outwards on social and cultural aspects of my personal experiences, and then inwards, exposing a vulnerable self, refracting cultural interpretations (Ellis and Bochner, 2000: 739) that are equivocal, uncertain and paradoxical. All of my interpretations are created in relationship, in between and on the borders of connections. To do this sort of work I need to be rigorously

Table 1.1 Autoethnography as feminist method

Autoethnography as a feminist method	Feminist autoethnographer	Responsibility of feminist autoethnographer	Feminist autoethnography in relations to others in the story
Creates transitional spaces, inhabiting the borderlands of embodied emotions	Becomes an embodied crossroads – who treats others with care, humility, honesty – and political and ethical sensitivity	To be a conduit – one who is cognizant of the complex connections between the socially enforced categories of gender, race, class and sexuality embedded in power relations	Their identities and experiences are uncertain, fluid, open to interpretation and able to be revised
Is an active demonstration of the 'personal is political'	Makes her private life public, her personal life political – a process coded by embodied affectivity	Personal revelations of vulnerability and shared precarity – tells and shows stories to become gifts	The boundaries between self and other break down as we help to open each other's eyes, hearts and minds to new political realities
Is feminist critical writing which is performative	Committed to the future of women	Bring into 'being new meanings and new subjectivities'	Stories that perform diversity, empower and enable, pointing towards women's liberation
Raises oppositional consciousness by exposing precarity	Is a member of the precariat and shares precarity with others	Helps other scholars to mend their wounds and see their vulnerabilities; to refute normative operations, pervasively racist, classist and heterosexist that decide in advance who counts as human and who does not	Precarity is shared, communal and embodied. It needs to be embraced and treasured. Cooperative politics emerge as connections are made.

self-aware, to be meticulously humble and most importantly, to be cognizant strictly of the complex connections between the socially coded categories of race, gender, class and sex and how as 'enforced differences'[5] these factors come to be embedded in power relations. All of this work needs to be performed in that borderland space – of 'in betweenness' where complex relational subjects are framed by embodiment, sexuality, affectivity, empathy and desire as core qualities (see Braidotti, 2013: 26). This space is unstable, always shifting and yet full of discovery and hope.

In this space, I treat identities and experiences as uncertain, fluid, open to interpretation and able to be revised (Adams and Holman Jones, 2011: 110). This transitional or in between fluid space creates for me a sense of empathy with those I study (Ellis, 2007). When telling an autoethnographic story, the story is not only mine – it is also co-owned with those in my story, sharing this borderland space. I am telling a story without borders, and yet I am an insider and an outsider – a living, embodied crossroads of words, flesh, emotions, interpretations and humanity. As this insider and outsider, I need to represent those people in my stories in the most compassionate ways possible – with care, humility and honesty and most importantly, with political and ethical sensitivity. At a crossroads and embodying one, I have the responsibility to show the way ahead, to make passage to understanding available and to allow stories to unfold with scrupulousness and honour. Autoethnography exposes the numerous possibilities we have in borderland spaces and how in these liberatory spaces we are able to make sense of our flexible and multiple identities. Although Judith Stacey (1991: 171) denies the possibility of 'a fully feminist ethnography', she argues for ethnographies that are 'partially feminist' and/or 'humble about the partiality of its ethnographic vision'. In a similar vein of thinking, Reinharz (1992: 260) contends that there is no politically correct feminist method, but a range of perspectives and this variety has been essential to the triumphs of international feminist scholarship. I am not interested in the question of whether or not there can be a feminist ethnography or a politically correct feminist method; rather, I am more concerned that in borderland spaces, autoethnography becomes an indicator of reliable feminist ethnography.

Autoethnography is an active demonstration of the 'personal is political'

Although sharing my autoethnography can be painful to me on a personal level, my stories can also be profoundly political, a view shared with other autoethnographers whose work I will summarise later. For example, in her search for Wonder Woman, Paige Averett (2009: 361) notes that autoethnography brings to mind the phrase from second-wave feminists: 'the personal is political'. Autoethnography for her is 'creative nonfiction', a 'conscious choice' and a 'process which does not include doing or writing research as one is taught in traditional academic settings'. Autoethnography has meaning for society 'because it is political and . . . intended to create change'. As a 'pointed truth' used to reveal the limitations of oppressive power structures within this society', autoethnography has 'the potential and power for change that exist through the practice of telling one's own story' (2009: 361).

Autoethnography as feminist method 7

When Robin Boylorn (2013) became a member of the person-of-colour scholar activist group, the Crunk Feminist Collective, she made her private life public, her personal life political. She revealed how 'Black feminism taught her to define herself for herself', 'gave her the framework to . . . privilege her everyday lived experiences as . . . relevant data for academic scholarship' and helped her embrace 'auto/ethnography' as it 'made sense in the context of her black feminist politics' (2013: 74).

Grace Giorgio (2009: 151) believes that telling and showing our stories become gifts because we create conversations that transcend our traumas. Writing as a survivor of lesbian battering, she says:

> when writing to heal ourselves, we help others to heal, we make our personal political' (p. 149) . . . In doing so, we turn our traumas into gifts . . . we witness the political dimensions to our own personal tragedies. By taking our personal hope and sharing it . . . for the sake of creating more hope, we commit a political act . . . transforming . . . understanding from personal to political (p. 159). Speaking one's truth or truths, through an autoethnographic lens, allows us to address the tensions between truths, whether personal or epistemological, in a political and hopeful act. It is political because it opens others' eyes to new realities of oppression and traumas; it is hopeful because it offers a chance for change (pp. 165–6).
>
> (Giorgio, 2009: 149–66)

Ruth Behar (1996: 26) noted that 'quests for personal narratives' and the breaking down of the boundaries between participant and observer were shifts 'in tandem with the feminist movement's assertion that the 'personal is political'. She contends that these shifts have changed the ways that 'scholars think about the subject as well as subjectivity of their work' (1996: 28). The implication is that personal revelation of vulnerability is acceptable in research writing. Indeed, Behar (1996: 2) says, 'a storyteller opens her heart to a story listener, recounting hurts that cut deep and raw into the gullies of the self'.

If we look back to the women's liberation movement of the 1960s and 1970s, we see that the principle, 'the personal is political' was embedded in feminist consciousness raising as a revolutionary practice. Linked with consciousness raising, we saw that being rational and emotional as well as thinking and feeling in feminist sociability was crucial. Indeed, during that time, Kathie Sarachild (1969: 202) wrote,

> Our feelings are telling us something from which we can learn . . . our feelings mean something worth analyzing . . . our feelings are saying something political, something reflecting fear that something bad will happen to us or hope, desire, knowledge that something good will happen to us. [. . .] let's share our feelings . . . . Our feelings will lead us to ideas and then to actions.

In another context, Sarachild (1975) describes one of the first consciousness raising groups in the East Coast women's liberation movement in the US. She talks about how within consciousness raising groups women's 'testimony is analysed' and how problems women think are 'their own private sorrows are shared by everyone in the group' (1975: 21). She asks, 'If all women share the same problem, how can it be personal?' and she answers, 'Women's pain is not personal, it's political' (1975: 21)

One of the first feminists to use the slogan 'the personal is political' was Carole Hanisch (2010), who reflects on the practice of consciousness raising:

> Young women . . . think that . . . 'consciousness raising is old hat' and that face-to-face group discussion isn't necessary to make further changes. Safely settling in behind computers and interacting on Facebook and other social networks – though certainly useful – has its limits. Consciousness-raising is timeless and limitless. It can update women's liberation thought and action in the hands of a new generation, but not if the goal is limited to self-expression. . . . it could even jumpstart a new era of radical change.

I included these discussions to reiterate the point that for feminist across generations 'the personal is political' and when this is coded by embodied affectivity, we are making politics.[6] Today, some feminists may see the notion, 'the personal is political' as an essentialist one (i.e. in which everything melds in together) or as a making truth claims (see Chapter 5). I justify a resurrection of this notion in that I am: (1) talking about breaking down boundaries between the academic and creative; (2) bringing myself in the middle of a postmodern discussion about language being an active agent and (3) demonstrating how to write situated knowledges of myself and the other into the text. This takes autoethnography far away from making truth claims. I want to shift the grounds of doing autobiography or memoir from autoethnography. I see the difference is between telling my story (i.e. autobiography) and theorising my story (i.e. autoethnography). I want to emphasize the different logics between these two methods.[7]

Thoughts and feelings derived from a specific configuration of feminist experiences are politically coded, and these thoughts and feelings help to open each other's eyes, hearts and minds to new political realities.[8] We are raising consciousness. In the 1960s and 1970s, consciousness raising meant helping oneself and others to become politically conscious. We gave testimony to our lives and bore witness to oppression, without interference from the presence of men. However, in today's world we would expect that consciousness raising transverses across genders, races, classes and sexualities, and that men, women and LGBTQI (lesbian, gay, bisexual, transgender, queer and intersex) people are able to provide political testimonies as well as create autoethnographies as political stories by expressing a mixture of rational calculations and emotions – their personal thoughts and feelings (see, for example, Chapter 1). For me, the vital issue here is emotions, feelings or embodied affectivity. In autoethnographies feelings are clear. I do not want to create a conventional binary between rationality and emotions or thoughts and feelings – an issue that will come up later in the chapter; instead, I want to emphasize that emotions, feelings and affect, which surface from our embodied experiences, have often been either ignored or downgraded in relationship to thinking, thoughts and rationality, especially within the academy. As I break down the boundaries between the academic and the creative in my autoethnographies, I discover that feelings are my greatest asset. For me, this is the reason why autoethnography, especially evocative autoethnography,[9] is a monumental method and one that has been criticized unfairly in my view.[10] Emphasizing affectivity, Ellis (2004: xix) says, autoethnography 'forms usually feature concrete action, emotion, embodiment, self-consciousness, and introspection portrayed in dialogue, scenes, characterization and plot'. I would add that these 'features' are not only methodologically but theoretically significant – they demonstrate sheer vitality as well as emancipation from antiquated methodological 'forms'. In short, by privileging embodied affectivity, autoethnography is an active demonstration of the 'personal is political' in today's complex, unequal world (Holman Jones, 2005).

Autoethnography is feminist critical writing which is performative and is committed to the future of women

In her analysis of what she terms 'feminist critical writing', Tania Modelski (1991: 47) argues that feminist critical writing is 'performative' because it embodies a promise – a 'commitment to the future', meaning a 'commitment to the future of women'. She contends further that in a liberatory context, 'feminist critical writing' aims at bringing into 'being new meanings and new subjectivities', 'not only 'what is' but also 'what has never been'. This complex performative dimension means 'doing something beyond restating already existent ideas and views, wherever these may happen to reside' (1991: 46).

For me, autoethnography fulfils this performative role. When I am telling my story, I am committed to transmitting my dream of feminism, helping my readers to amalgamate feminist ways of thinking and practice into their daily lives. In her now classic article, 'Theory as liberatory practice', bell hooks (1991: 8–9) bemoans the fact that there is 'so much feminist writing produced and yet so little feminist theory that strives to speak to women, men and children about ways we might transform our lives via a conversion to feminist politics, to feminist practice'. I don't want my autoethnography work to be disempowering and disabling; rather, I want my autoethnographies to point toward women's liberation. This may sound old fashioned and grandiose, but I agree with bell hooks (1991: 11) when she says:

> I am grateful to the many women and men who dare to create theory from the location of pain and struggle, who courageously expose wounds to give us their experience to teach and guide, as a means to chart new theoretical journeys. Their work is liberatory. It not only enables us to remember and recover ourselves, it charges and challenges us to renew our commitment to an active, inclusive feminist struggle. We have still to collectively make feminist revolution. I am grateful that we are collectively searching as feminist thinkers/theorists for ways to make this movement happen. Our search leads us back to where it all began, to that moment when an individual woman or child, who may have thought she was all alone, began feminist uprising, began to name her practice, indeed began to formulate theory from lived experience.

Where in today's world can we find theoretical and methodological work that really challenges the status quo, privileging whiteness, men, heteronormativity, the able bodied, the 1 per cent rich, Western ways of thinking, the global North, etc.? What is wrong with the dream of liberation in our neoliberal world, which creates a maze of deep inequalities and profound human suffering? What is iniquitous with using feminist theory to bring about feminist change? In this context, I want to refer again to bell hooks (1991: 8) who says:

> Within revolutionary feminist movements, within revolutionary black liberation struggles, we must continually claim theory as necessary practice within a holistic framework of liberatory activism. We must do more than call attention to ways theory is misused. We must do more than critique the conservative and at times reactionary uses some academic women make of feminist theory. We must actively work to call attention to the importance of creating a theory that can advance renewed feminist movements, particularly highlighting that theory which seeks to further feminist opposition to sexism, and sexist oppression.

When I use autoethnography as a feminist method, I am creating theory by my commitment to the future of all women and women's liberation. Thus, when sharing my stories, I want to expose new feminist meanings and new feminist subjectivities. I want to move beyond 'restating already existent ideas and views'. Thus, my autoethnographies may show commonality between women but these stories also perform diversity. We see empathy, caring and love but we also see hate, insensitivity, discomfort, vindictiveness and indifference to other's feelings. Although we see sisterhood or the solidarity of women based on shared conditions, experiences or concerns in these stories, there is also present animosity or hatred towards women and all of the oppressed amongst us. My stories live in the real world and I do not frame them in a feminist utopia; however, in attempting to show new meanings and new subjectivities, I try in my stories to empower readers. I want to show them what perhaps has never been in their minds – to give hope and solace, possibilities in the face of social injustice and, more importantly, sheer cruelty. This is a difficult task but autoethnography allows me to use my imagination in a creative way to envision a future – a human or rather post-human future, which is possible and believable.

As feminist critical writing, autoethnography can be simultaneously 'performative and utopian, pointing toward the freer world it is in the process of inaugurating' (Modelski, 1991: 48). Furthermore, in considering the politicization of the performative, Butler (Butler and Athanasiou, 2013: 101) contends that in today's world, 'performativity takes place when the uncounted prove to be reflexive and start to count themselves . . . exercising . . . a "right" to existence. They start to matter'. Butler's co-author, Athanasiou (Butler and Athanasiou, 2013: 40) argues that 'unsettling the hegemony of neoliberal capitalism involves opening up conceptual, discursive, affective and political spaces for enlarging our economic and political imaginary'. In this context, autoethnography helps those uncounted matter, opens up those spaces for enlarging our economic and political imaginary and calls for political responsiveness embedded in performativity. Autoethnography supports radical performance, which disturbs established 'norms of intelligibility'.[11] Autoethnographers aim to uncover, if not upset, the normative, hegemonic and prevailing ways we analyse human relationships as academics.

Autoethnography helps to raise oppositional consciousness by exposing precarity

Related to the earlier discussion, precarity is closely related to performativity. Indeed, Butler (Butler and Athanasiou, 2013: 101) contends that

> the exercise of the right to existence is something that happens within the context of precarity and takes form as a precarious exercise that seeks to overcome its own precarity . . . Performativity works within precarity and against its differential allocation . . . Performativity names that unauthorized exercise of a right to existence that propels the precarious into political life.

Autoethnographers are often propelled into political life when they tell stories of precarious, vulnerable lives (see, for example, Adams and Holman Jones, 2011; Boylorn, 2013; Camangian, 2010; Cole Robinson and Clardy, 2010; Crawley, 2012; Ellis, 2004, 2007, 2009; Ettorre, 2010; Griffin, 2012; Pathak, 2010; Ronai and Ellis, 1989; Shomali, 2012; Spry, 2001; Tomaselli et al., 2013; Vidal-Ortiz, 2004).

When I write as an autoethnographer, I see myself as active in political life as well as a member of the precariat who wants to 'mend wounds by remembering' (Vannini, 2008: 165). Hopefully, I am able to help other scholars to mend their wounds, see their own vulnerabilities and become politicised. Since the beginning of the millennium, academic studies on the links between vulnerability, precarity, social justice and human rights have grown. Broadly speaking, if precarity is a constitutive aspect of our lives, we need a clear understanding of what this means. In the next discussion, I will summarise and outline how key feminist scholars define precarity.

Isabell Lorey (2012: 164–5) speaks of three dimensions of 'the precarious':

- 'Precarity' as a category of order that denotes social positionings of insecurity and hierarchization, which accompanies processes of Othering;
- 'Governmental precarization', designating not only working and living conditions but also ways of subjectivation, embodiment, and agency; and
- 'Precariousness' as a relational condition of social being that cannot be avoided and is intertwined with the other two dimensions.

Drawing from moral philosophy and ideas on ethical obligations and agency, Judith Butler (2012: 170) elaborates on Lorey's definition of precarity. Butler claims that 'our precarity is to a large extent dependent upon the organization of economic and social relationships; the presence or absence of sustaining infrastructures; and social and political institutions'. For her, precarity is 'indissociable from that dimension of politics that addresses the organization and protection of bodily needs'; precarity 'exposes our sociality, the fragile and necessary dimensions of our interdependency'.[12] Butler (2012:170) contends that, 'We have to start from this shared condition of precarity (not as existential fact, but as a social condition of political life) in order to refute those normative operations, pervasively racist, that decide in advance who counts as human and who does not'.

In observing the effects of precarity on contemporary life, Lauren Berlant (2007) talks about 'slow death' that 'elaborates how precarity is socialized into the intensification of the "on-going work of living"' (Puar, 2012: 162). For Berlant (2007: 754) slow death 'refers to the physical wearing out of a population and the deterioration of people in that population that is very nearly a defining condition of their experience and historical existence. The general emphasis . . . is on 'the phenomenon of mass physical attenuation under global/national regimes of capitalist structural subordination and governmentality'. In another context, Berlant (2012: 171) contends that 'the situation of precarity . . . is the situation of relationality itself, insofar as our dependencies are vulnerabilities'. It is '. . . a situation of aggression – because of needs whose demands are unmet'.

What we see from these definitions from feminist scholars is that 'precarity is not solely intrinsic to life in its individual existence but also in and through its collective repetition across lives' (Nyong'o, 2013: 157–8). Precarity is shared, communal and embodied (Butler and Athanasiou, 2013). Although precarity may be the new buzz word in feminist theory, I see it as the 'red line' throughout all of my autoethnographies – reminding me of precarity's 'collective repetition across lives' – 'situations of relationality', emerging through the thinking and feeling with our research stories. Precarity teaches me, as an autoethnographer and feminist thinker, not only that we have vulnerabilities and are utterly dependent upon each other but also that this dependency, this sense of precariousness is a vital force – a great strength.

An awareness of precarity allows us to be cognizant of our post-human condition and move towards more balanced, embodied, emotional and rational lives. Precarity's positive contribution is that it allows us to value vulnerability without accepting social injustice, interdependency without fomenting hate and hope without wallowing in despair. If precarity is a social condition of political life, we need to be aware of it, embrace it and treasure it. Most importantly, we need to be attentive to 'precarity that inhabits the microspaces of daily life, in the spaces in which individuals think and feel and interact' (Ettlinger, 2007: 324). This is where autoethnography is able to reveal its methodological strength – this attention to precarity as it infiltrates the microspaces of our lives. Precarity is 'unbounded'. To think otherwise would be for us to fall into an essentialist trap (2007: 320).

When we do autoethnography, we remember that our experiences of precarity 'constitute evolving and intersecting governmentalities' (2007: 320). In order to survive, we need, as Ettlinger (2007: 321–4) contends, to understand the 'everydayness of conditions that give rise to precarity' and take a non-essentialist stance. We need to refuse separation of spheres of life into politics, economics, family, work and so on, and to reject the separation of rationality and emotions. Importantly, a focus on the relation between rationality and emotions allows oppositional consciousness to take shape. For Ettlinger (2007: 325) whether or not our oppositional politics connect with others is uncertain.

However, as an autoethnographer, if I am able to make connections with others, cooperative politics will emerge in my autoethnographies. Thus, I am able to 'permit resistance to a governmentality by manipulating it and working to develop a new, positive governmentality that connects with the values of everyday citizens' (2007: 335). If precarity is a constitutive aspect of many people's lives, oppositional consciousness along with cooperative politics are needed in today's ever-changing, uncertain and unpredictable world.

Feminist autoethnography and the core ideals of autoethnography

This chapter began when I gave a brief explanation of autoethnography and agreed with Allen and Piercy (2005: 156) that in feminist autoethnography we tell the stories of those who are marginalized and make good use of our experience. I extended this argument further by discussing four ways in which autoethnography can be feminist method. Now I want to focus attention on the four core ideals of autoethnography as discussed by Adams *et al.* (2014: 607–13) in their excellent text, *Autoethnography: Understanding Qualitative Research*. I will examine each core ideal separately and discuss how each ideal is consistent with a feminist approach to autoethnography.

Recognizing the limits of scientific knowledge (what can be known or explained), particularly regarding identities, lives and relationships, and creating nuanced, complex and specific accounts of personal/cultural experience

Feminists have been aware for decades that our bodies are situated in space and time and that 'the way gender gets constructed interactionally will vary with the context' (i.e. what is being talked about, with whom, in what social setting and for what purposes) (Cameron, 2009: 5). In this context, Sara Ahmed (2006) teaches us that bodies take shape as they move through the world directing themselves toward or away from objects and others. She contends that being 'orientated' means feeling at home, knowing where one stands, or having certain objects within reach. Our orientations affect what is proximate to our bodies or what can be grasped. For Ahmed, a queer phenomenology reveals how social relations are organized spatially, how queerness disturbs and rearranges these relations by not following the normative paths, and how a politics of disorientation puts additional objects within reach, those that might at first glance seem askew. Autoethnography embraces queer phenomenology not only by creating nuanced accounts of my cultural experiences but also by not following my rearranged paths of knowing. Employing a sort of queer phenomenology, Joshi (2007: 2–3) contends that autoethnography is an intervention into Western epistemology, an epistemology that favours 'cognitive, intellectual understanding above all else'. He contends that autoethnography introduces the goals of 'visceral response and emotional empathy'

14 *Autoethnography as feminist method*

and autoethnographers consider the sensual–emotional and the intellectual–analytic registers to be opposites that cancel each other out. He wants us to experience these registers as 'intertwining braids that flow together to yield a deeper, clearer stream of understanding'. In this sense, by creating politics of disorientation, autoethnography fashions feminist, queer spaces in which I am able to craft my knowledge from disorientation as well as employ an 'epistemology of contradictions' (O'Brien, 2010). In the end, as a feminist, I am able to conserve a more well-rounded apprehension as well as comprehension of my experience.

Connecting personal (insider) experience, insights and knowledge to larger (relational, cultural, political) conversations, contexts and conventions

We saw in the previous discussions how autoethnography as a method can be an active demonstration of the 'personal is political'. Holman Jones (2005) makes a clear connection between the two, while Crawley (2012) envisages autoethnography as 'feminist self-interview'. Thus, in considering the intersections of feminism and autoethnography, I am able to use past experiences to connect the personal and the political. In her book, *Feminist Fieldwork Analysis*, Kleinman (2007) organises her text around five principles, one of which is the 'personal is political'. She contends that this principle demonstrates the 'importance of linking participants' emotions with power relations' (2007: 10). Although as a feminist I will be a participant in my autoethnography, my stories are the result of my explicit reflections on my personal experience. Allen and Piercy (2005: 159) contend that I am able to 'break the outside circle of conventional social science and confront, court and coax that aching pain or haunting memory that I do not understand about my experience'. Autoethnography is ideally suited for feminists who want to be self-reflexive[13] and humble about their own positions in the world. However, problems can arise even for the most diligent feminist autoethnographer. Here, I ask 'How do we see ourselves interacting with our worlds, worlds which may become synonymous with 'in the field'? For example, when speaking of personal ethnography, Crawford (1996: 163) talks about the most problematic issue for him when doing fieldwork: 'the deliberate interference it entails' and its 'intrusiveness'.

In this context, autoethnography may be viewed as focusing 'on the wrong side of the power divide' (Delamont, 2007: 4). Indeed, Atkinson (2006: 403) contends that although these personalised, experiential accounts (i.e. autoethnography) may involve 'social criticism', this 'does not excuse their essentially self-absorbed nature: the personal is political, but the personal does not exhaust or subsume all aspects of the political'. Yes, that is perhaps clear – if you are not a feminist and/or do not value emotions.

As an autoethnographer, I may make interpretations of another's behaviour without asking specifically if I can. But my interpretations need to be based on my feminist reflexivity. In this context, there is a tension that informs all progressive social change research: the tension between our political sensibilities and goals and our intellectual mission to produce reliable knowledge (Avishai *et al.*, 2012:

394). In responding to that tension, as feminist researchers we should incorporate 'institutional reflexivity on feminism itself as part of our ethnographic practice' (2012: 394). This means that when I am 'in the field' of my life, I may have a highly politicized, feminist agenda, but this agenda should not lead to a blurring of the personal and the political (see Jewkes, 2011); rather, I need to recognize my feminist subjectivity as a valuable resource that affects every aspect of my research process. As an autoethnographer, I recognize that I am a feminist researcher, a sensitive methodologist, a queer phenomenologist and a cultural being – all positions that I insist do not take my politics for granted; rather, my politics are shaped in my autoethnographies by a merging, sometimes uneasy and sometimes easy, of my emotions, intellect, bodily sensations and sensibilities in interactions with others.

Answering the call to narrative and storytelling and placing equal importance on intellect/knowledge and aesthetics/artistic craft

The leading proponents of autoethnography – Ellis (1991, 1995, 1999, 2000) Richardson (2000a, 2000b, 2000c, 2003) and Bochner (2000, 2001, 2003) – share a consensus: autoethnography should be evaluated through two lenses, science and art. Autoethnography makes a substantive, aesthetic contribution to understanding social life, it demonstrates reflexivity and has an impact on the reader (Richardson, 2000a). 'Conversations' should 'feel' real to life and have the power to stimulate social action (Ellis, 2000; 274). As an autoethnographer, I extract meaning from experience rather than depict experience as it was lived (Bochner, 2000). The intention, shape and rapport of my artistic piece should emulate the emotional and scientific commitment of a triumvirate: me, as the author, the story and the reader. For feminists engaged in autoethnography, merging art and science is crucial. When I write my autoethnographies, I want 'to write from the heart, bring the first person in my work and merge art and science' (Ellis and Bochner, 2000). I want my readers to be able to feel with my story and engage with my story on an emotional level. Like other autoethnographers (Tedlock, 2000: 468), I attempt to clarify and authenticate my self-image and feelings. As a feminist researcher, I become the epistemological and ontological nexus upon which the research process turns (Spry, 2001: 711). Crafting my autoethnographic stories not only demands reflexivity but also critical intelligence combined with a sense of my acute embodied emotions. In effect, as a feminist, I create an atmosphere of epistemological intimacy (Smith, 2005) but with an awareness that I am creating art as well as 'doing' feminist science. Leavy (2012: 517) offers an excellent explanation of artistic work and I would like to apply this to feminist autoethnography. She says:

> Artistic enterprises offer a different lens onto social experience (Richardson, 2001), promote reflection and negotiation, open multiple meanings, and make social research more accessible to diverse audiences (Leavy, 2009). Thomas (2001) notes, 'Art as inquiry has the power to evoke, to inspire, to spark the emotions, to awaken visions and imaginings, and to transport others to new

worlds' (2001: 274). Perhaps more than anything else, the products of arts-based research have the potential to tap into emotions and build resonance.

Along with a deep awareness of emotions, feminist autoethnographers need to embrace what Sotirin (2010: 2) calls the 'radical specificity of lived experience' – 'the plethora of sensations, vibrations, movements, and intensities that constitute both our world and ourselves (Grosz, 2001: 171)'. In answering the call to narrative and storytelling, I, as a feminist autoethnographer, maintain a balance between my own self-reflexivity, my personal knowledge and my sense of aesthetics. I craft my life experiences as a story, but a story that is able to move others emotionally and aesthetically. This task may not be easy for me. It demands perseverance and personal integrity.

Attending to the ethical implications of their work for themselves, their participants, and their readers/audiences

Autoethnography demands a profound awareness of ethics. In my travels around academia, I have heard horror stories of how a particular colleague wanted to write an autoethnography in order to expose or to take revenge concerning wrongdoings at a workplace, the vagaries of a difficult divorce, fights with siblings, etc. Immediately I think that this is not what autoethnography is about – a venting of bad or negative feelings. As a feminist autoethnographer, my end goal is consistently to use autoethnography as feminist method in which the feminist concerns of ethic and care occupy a central place in my stories. Basically, I need to be ethically accountable to methodological principles of how I portray others. Whether the source of my data is personal diaries, memoirs, taped discussions, poetry, performance, or sheer memory through emotional recall, etc.,[14] I am answerable to others in my story. There are no research participants as outlined by the remit of Research Ethics Committees (Beyleveld *et al.*, 2002) or anyone identified as a conventional respondent from whom gaining informed consent is necessarily required (Crow *et al.*, 2004). Thus, seeking ethical approval may not be not necessary.[15] Nevertheless, whenever possible, I inform all significant others of my accounts either in writing or verbally. However, there are instances where I may not inform others.[16] Without informing the 'others' in my story, I will protect consistently the anonymity of all of them by way of consistently changing names of people and places. Talking to others who are involved in my story is important. I gain self-assurance, while they gain important information as well as the opportunity to consider that understanding my experiences may enrich their own lives. When I follow this line of thinking, I feel as if I am able to find my feminist voice. When I write my social science prose, I keep in my mind what Ellis (2007: 3) says that because autoethnography concerns the researcher's self and relations with other selves in various spaces, the blurring of boundaries and the blurring of roles, this inevitably involves relational ethics.

When I speak about ethics as a feminist autoethnographer, I speak of having a sense of *emotional compassing*, which means that I use my embodied emotions to guide me in composing my stories *in relation to others*. A range of emotions may be involved and finding this range may not be emotionally comfortable or comforting for me. Emotional compassing demands that I go through difficult feelings or emotions. For example, I may be telling a story in which I was deeply hurt by an other or others. I may go through a range of feelings from anger, hate and resentment to compassion, forgiveness, mercy, etc. But, it is always best to see an other or others with a sympathetic or lenient lens and to write my autoethnography after going through a range of emotions. Emotional compassing helps me to write my autoethnography with a deep sense of 'Hesed.'[17] Thus, my feminist autoethnographies demands kindness to others as well as myself. I am not making truth claims in my stories. I am merely representing 'my truths' which others may or may not see as their truths in my stories. As an autoethnographer, my end goal is consistently to use autoethnography as feminist method in which the feminist concerns of ethics and care occupy a central place in my stories. Basically, I need to be ethically accountable to methodological principles of how I portray others. Through my emotional compassing, I embody Hesed and am sensitive to my feminist 'I'.

The structure of this book

There are five remaining chapters in this book. Chapters 1 through 4 contain autoethnographic stories that explain my career as a lesbian feminist academic and what my career involved during the years from 1978 to 2016 (see Chapter 1: Being a 'sexual pervert' in academia); a story of being ill as a menopausal woman (Chapter 2: Finding my feminist voice through an illness story: 'an old female body confronts a thyroid problem'); doing drugs use research in the drugs field with women who use drugs (Chapter 3: Doing feminist autoethnography with drug-using women); and a story of being intimidated in retirement by colleagues with whom I was co-authoring a book (Chapter 4: '*She wrote it but look what she wrote*'). With the exception of Chapter 4, all chapters include autoethnographic analyses of my stories. In the final chapter, Chapter 5: Sensitising the feminist 'I', I analyse Chapter 4 alongside other chapters and employ the four criteria that I developed in using autoethnography as a feminist method in this introductory chapter. I want to demonstrate clearly how feminist thinking can facilitate an autoethnographic approach. In this context, remembering Giorgio's (2009) work is instructive. In this transmission of a feminist vision through autoethnography 'our stories become gifts' – gifts that are transformative and full of promise. The aim of this book is to further a feminist understanding of autoethnography and to help other feminists to tell their own stories and sensitise their own feminist 'I'.

Notes

1 Here, Benhabib (1990: 187) means that a self is the 'protagonist of activity' and can only be identified by who he/she is by their actions. Human actions live in the 'narratives of those who perform them and the narratives of those who understand, interpret, and recall them'.
2 I had a fascinating discussion with postgraduate students at Rensselaer Polytechnic Institute where we discussed autoethnography as a writing genre as well as a method of research.

18 *Autoethnography as feminist method*

3   In this context, Stanley goes on to say, '. . . (the) "self" does not exist in isolation from interrelationship with other selves and other lives; it is grounded in the material reality of everyday life, and a key part of the constitution of this material reality is formed by the narrations of selves and others that figure so importantly in everyday talk as well as being a "hidden" component of much academic writing' (1993: 133).

4   I would argue that the boundaries between autoethnography and (critical) autobiography can be at times blurred. Here, I am grateful to Konstantina Poursanidou for pointing out 'critical autobiography' to me and making me aware of the excellent text by Church (1995), *Forbidden Narratives: Critical Autobiography as Social Science* among others.

5   Rosi Braidotti (2013) talks about how within 'an intersectional analysis', we need to look at 'the methodological parallelisms of these factors . . . without flattening out any differences between them but rather investing politically in the question of their complex interaction' (2013: 27, footnote 4).

6   In a *Washington Post* article, 'Betty Friedan to Beyoncé: Today's generation embraces feminism on its own terms', the authors (Shenin *et al.*, 2016) note that ' "The personal is political," went one popular slogan for Second Wave feminism, and some younger feminists have revived the slogan to reflect their belief that pursuing individual freedoms is very much a political exercise and to defend themselves against criticism from older feminists that they aren't political enough'.

7   I am very grateful for the postgraduate students at Tema Genus-Interdisciplinary Gender Studies, Linköping University, Sweden for their helpful insights in my discussion on 'Autoethnography as an active demonstration of the "personal is political" ' when I was visiting them for a seminar on 20 January 2015.

8   Here, we need to recognise that for some feminists, autoethnography could be described as a 'perfect method' because it emphasizes not only the importance of one's subjective experience but also presents an objective view of what happens. Thus, the subjective is as important as the objective when creating an autoethnographic perspective. I am grateful to Imma, my partner, for discussing this aspect of feminist autoethnography with me.

9   See Bochner and Ellis (2016) for a full expose of evocative autoethnography.

10 For example, proposing analytical authoethnography as the best option *vis-à-vis* evocative authoethnography (i.e. authoethnographys using feelings), Anderson (2006: 373) is critical of evocative authoethnography which 'has obscured recognition of the compatibility of authoethnography with more traditional practices'. Also, Atkinson (2006: 402–3) sees problems with evocative authoethnography which 'stems from a tendency to promote ethnographic research on writing on the basis of its experiential value, its evocative qualities, and its personal commitments rather than its scholarly purpose, its theoretical bases, and its disciplinary contributions'. He argues that 'the fact that these personalised, experiential accounts are sometimes justified in terms of social criticism does not excuse their essentially self-absorbed nature: the personal is political, but the personal does not exhaust or subsume all aspects of the political' (2006: 403). I see the problem for these thinkers as the incursion of feelings into the academy.

11 In this context, Athanasiou (Butler and Athanasiou, 2013: 92) contends that 'we are performatively constituted and de-constituted by and through our relations to the others among whom we live, as well as by and through particular regulatory norms that secure cultural intelligibility'. We are 'structurally dependent on social norms that we neither choose nor control' and there exists a 'different and differential manner in which the anxieties and the excitements of relationality are socially distributed'. Basically we all struggle against social norms in some fashion – norms related to the normalization of race, class, gender, sexuality, nationality, age, etc. As implied in the epigraph, feminist researchers, need to attend to these subtleties of inequalities (in race, class, gender, sexual orientation, ability, age, etc.) and how we are socially programmed by them.

12 'Whether explicitly stated or not, every political effort to manage populations involves a tactical distribution of precarity, more often than not articulated through an unequal

distribution of precarity, one that depends upon dominant norms regarding *whose life is grievable* and worth protecting, and *whose life is ungrievable*, or marginally or episodically grievable – a life that is, in that sense, already lost in part or in whole, and thus less worthy of protection and sustenance' Butler (2012: 170, emphasis added).
13 See Chapter 3 for a further discussion of self-reflexivity in relationship to autoethnography with women drug users.
14 See Ellis's (1999) article 'Heartful ethnography' where she discusses the importance of emotional recall. Ellis (1999: 675) defines emotional recall when the researcher imagines being back in key events emotionally and physically. It is embedded in sociological introspection, a process that can be accomplished in dialogue with the self and represented in the form of narratives (see also Ellis, 1991).
15 Denshire (2014: 841) notes that 'devices that are intended to protect participants' identities in auto-ethnographic accounts include fictionalizing (Clough, 2002) and the use of symbolic equivalents (Yalom, 1991). Protective writing devices such as a *nom de plume* (Morse, 2000), composite characterization (Ellis, 2007) and pseudonyms (Chang, 2008) can be used in an effort to respect the privacy of those portrayed in an auto-ethnographic narrative'.
16 This happened recently when I decided if I did contact these 'others' in my story, it would be a hurtful process. Because I interpreted the basis of our relationship as hurtful, probably both ways, I decided I did not want to continue 'the hurt cycle'.
17 That is, Heced or Chesed from the Hebrew word meaning 'loving-kindness' or 'loyal love' but a 'faithful love in action' aware of the sufferings of others (see http://preceptaustin.org/lovingkindness-definition_of_hesed.htm; accessed 4 March 2016).

References

Adams, T. E. and Holman Jones, S. (2011) Telling stories: reflexivity, queer theory, and autoethnography. *Cultural Studies – Critical Methodologies* 11, 2: 108–16.

Adams, T. E., Holman Jones, S. and Ellis, C. (2014) *Autoethnography: Understanding Qualitative Research*. Oxford: Oxford University Press (Kindle edition).

Ahmed, S. (2006) *Queer Phenomenology: Orientations, Objects, Others*. Durham, NC: Duke University Press.

Allen, K. R. and Piercy, F. P. (2005) 'Feminist autoethnography'. In: Sprenkle, D. H. and Piercy, F. P. (eds.) *Research Methods in Family Therapy*. New York, NY: Guilford Press, pp. 155–69.

Anderson, L. (2006) Analytic Autoethnography. *Journal of Contemporary Ethnography* 35, 4: 373–95.

Anzaldua, G. (1987) *Borderlands, La Frontera: The New Mestiza*. San Francisco, CA: Aunt Lute Books.

Arendt, H. (1998) *The Human Condition*. 2nd edn. Chicago, IL: University of Chicago Press.

Atkinson, P. (2006) Rescuing autoethnography. *Journal of Contemporary Ethnography* 35, 4: 400–4.

Averett, P. (2009) The search for Wonder Woman: an autoethnography of feminist identity. *Affilia* 24, 4: 360–8.

Avishai, O., Gerber, L. and Randles, J. (2012) The feminist ethnographer's dilemma: reconciling progressive research agendas with fieldwork realities. *Journal of Contemporary Ethnography* 42, 4: 394–426.

Bartleet, B. L. and Ellis, C. (2009) *Making Autoethnography Sing/Making Music Personal*. Samford Valley, QLD: Australian Academic Press.

Behar, R. (1996) *The Vulnerable Observer: Anthropology that Breaks Your Heart*. Boston, MA: Beacon Press.

Bell, S. E. (2000) 'Experiences of illness and narrative understandings'. In Brown, P. (ed.), *Perspectives in Medical Sociology*. Prospect Heights, IL: Waveland Press, pp. 130–45.

Benhabib, S. (1990) Hannah Arendt and the redemptive power of narrative. *Social Research* 57, 1: 167–96.

Berlant, L. (2007) Slow Death (Sovereignty, Obesity, Lateral Agency). *Critical Inquiry* 33, 4: 754–80.

Berlant, L. (2012) Precarity talk: a virtual roundtable with Lauren Berlant, Judith Butler, Bojana Cvejic, Isabell Lorey, Jasbir Puar and Ana Vujanovic; edited by Jasbir Puar. *TDR: The Drama Review* 56, 4: 163–77.

Beyleveld, D., Brownsword, R. and Wallace, S. (2002) 'Independent ethics committees in the United Kingdom'. In Lebeer, G. (ed.), *Ethical Function in Hospital Ethics Committees*. Amsterdam: IOS Press, pp. 111–23.

Bochner, A. (2000) Criteria against ourselves. *Qualitative Inquiry* 6, 2: 266–72.

Bochner, A. (2001) Narratives' virtues. *Qualitative Inquiry* 7, 2: 131–57.

Bochner, A. (2003) An introduction to the arts and narrative research: art as inquiry. *Qualitative Inquiry* 9, 4: 506–14.

Bochner, A. and Ellis, C. (2016) *Evocative Autoethnography: Writing Lives and Telling Stories*. New York, NY: Routledge.

Bowring, F. (2013) *Hannah Arendt: A Critical Introduction* (Modern European Thinkers). London: Pluto Press (Kindle edition).

Boylorn, R. M. (2013) Blackgirl blogs, auto/ethnography, and crunk feminism. *Liminalities: A Journal of Performance Studies* 9, 2: 73–82.

Braidotti, R. (2013) *The Posthuman*. Cambridge: Polity Press.

Butler, J. (2012) Precarity talk: a virtual roundtable with Lauren Berlant, Judith Butler, Bojana Cvejic, Isabell Lorey, Jasbir Puar and Ana Vujanovic; edited by Jasbir Puar. *TDR: The Drama Review* 56, 4: 163–77.

Butler, J. and Athanasiou, A. (2013) *Dispossession: The Performative in the Political*, Cambridge: Polity Press.

Camangian, P. (2010) Starting with self: teaching autoethnography to foster critically caring literacies. *Research in the Teaching of English* 45, 2: 179–204. Available at www.jstor.org/stable/40997089 (accessed 6 April 2016).

Cameron, D. (2009) 'Theoretical issues for the study of gender and spoken interaction'. In Pichler, P. and Eppler, E. (eds.), *Gender and Spoken Interaction*. Houndmills, UK: Palgrave Macmillan, pp. 1–17.

Chang, H. (2008) *Autoethnography as Method: Developing Qualitative Inquiry*. Walnut Creek, CA: Left Coast Press.

Church, K. (1995) *Forbidden Narratives: Critical Autobiography as Social Science*. London: Gordon and Breach.

Clarke, A. E. (2005) *Situational Analysis: Grounded Theory After the Postmodern Turn*. London: Sage Publications.

Cole Robinson, C. and Clardy, P. (eds.) (2010) *Tedious Journeys: Autoethnography by Women of Color in Academe*. New York, NY: Peter Lang.

Cosslett, T., Lury, C. and Summerfield, P. (eds.) (2000) *Feminism & Autobiography: Texts, Theories and Methods*. London: Routledge.

Crawford, L. (1996) Personal ethnography. *Communication Monographs* 63, 2: 163.

Crawley, S. L. (2012) 'Autoethnography as feminist self-interview'. In Gubrium, J. F., Holstein, Marvasti, J. A. and McKinney, K. D. (eds.), *The Sage Handbook of Interview Research*. 2nd edn. Thousand Oaks, CA: Sage Publications, pp. 143–60.

Crow, G., Charles, V., Heath, S. and Wiles, R. (2004) 'Informed consent and the research process: following rules or striking balances'. Paper presented at the Annual Conference of the British Sociological Association, York, UK, 22–24 March.

Delamont, S. (2007) Arguments against auto-ethnography. *Qualitative Researcher* 4, February: 2–4. Available at www.cardiff.ac.uk/socsi/qualiti/QualitativeResearcher/QR_Issue4_Feb07.pdf (accessed 2 March 2016).

Denshire, S. (2014) On auto-ethnography. *Current Sociology Review* 62, 6: 831–50.

Ellis, C. (1991) Sociological introspection and emotional experience. *Symbolic Interaction* 14, 1: 23–50.

Ellis, C. (1995) *Final Negotiations: A Story of Love, Loss and Chronic Illness*. Philadelphia, PA: Temple University Press.

Ellis, C. (1999) Heartful ethnography. *Qualitative Health Research* 9, 5: 669–83.

Ellis, C. (2000) Creating criteria: an ethnographic short story. *Qualitative Inquiry* 6, 2: 273–7.

Ellis, C. (2004) *The Ethnographic I: A Methodological Novel about Teaching and Doing Autoethnography*. Walnut Creek, CA: Alta Mira.

Ellis, C. (2007) Telling secrets, revealing lives: relational ethics in research with intimate others. *Qualitative Inquiry* 13, 1: 3–29.

Ellis, C. (2009) *Revision: Autoethnographic Reflections on Life and Work*. Walnut Creek, CA: Left Coast Press.

Ellis, C. and Bochner, A. (1996) *Composing Ethnography: Alternative Forms of Qualitative Writing*. Walnut Creek, CA: Alta Mira.

Ellis, C. and Bochner, A. (2000) 'Autoethnography, personal narrative, reflexivity: researcher as subject'. In Denzin, N. and Lincoln, Y. (eds.), *Handbook of Qualitative Research*. Thousand Oaks: Sage Publications, pp. 733–68.

Ettlinger, N. (2007) Precarity unbound. *Alternatives* 32: 319–40.

Ettorre, E. (2010) Nuns, dykes, drugs and gendered bodies: an autoethnography of a lesbian feminist's journey through 'good time' sociology. *Sexualities* 13, 3: 295–315.

Forber-Pratt, A. J. (2015) 'You're going to do what?'. Challenges of autoethnography in the academy. *Qualitative Inquiry* 21, 9: 821–35.

Giorgio, G. (2009) Traumatic truths and the gift of telling. *Qualitative Inquiry* 15, 1: 149–67.

Griffin, R. A. (2012) 'I AM an angry black woman: black feminist autoethnography, voice, and resistance. *Women's Studies in Communication*. 35, 2: 138–57.

Hanisch, C. (2010) Women's liberation consciousness-raising: then and now. *On the Issues Magazine: A Magazine of Feminist, Progressive Thinking* (Spring) Available at www.ontheissuesmagazine.com/2010spring/2010spring_Hanisch.php (accessed 1 November 2014).

Holman Jones, S. (2005) 'Autoethnography: making the personal political'. In Denzin, N. K. and Lincoln, Y. (eds.), *The Sage Handbook of Qualitative Research*. 3rd edn. Thousand Oaks, CA: Sage Publications, pp. 763–91.

hooks, b. (1991) Theory as liberatory practice. *Yale Journal of Law and Feminism* 4, 1: 1–12.

Jewkes, Y. (2011) Autoethnography and emotion as intellectual resources: doing prison research differently. *Qualitative Inquiry* 18, 1: 63–75.

Joshi, S. (2007) Homo sutra: disrobing desire in the adult cinema. *Journal of Creative Work* 1, 2. Available at www.scientificjournals.org/journals2007/articles/1188.pdf (accessed 31 March 2016).

Katz Rothman, B. (2005) The I in sociology. *Chronicle of Higher Education*, 22 April.

Katz Rothman, B. (2007) Writing ourselves in sociology. *Methodological Innovations Online* 2, 1: 11–16.

Kleinman, S. (2003) 'Feminist fieldworker: connecting research, teaching, and memoir'. In Glassner, B. and Hertz, R. (eds.), *Our Studies, Ourselves: Sociologists' Lives and Work*. New York, NY: Oxford University Press, pp. 215–32.

Kleinman, S. (2007) *Feminist Fieldwork Analysis*. Qualitative Research Methods Volume 51. London: Sage Publications.

Leavy, P. (2012) Fiction and the feminist academic novel. *Qualitative Inquiry* 18, 6: 516–22.

Lorey, I. (2012) Precarity talk: a virtual roundtable with Lauren Berlant, Judith Butler, Bojana Cvejic, Isabell Lorey, Jasbir Puar and Ana Vujanovic; edited by Jasbir Puar. *TDR: The Drama Review* 56, 4: 163–77.

Maynes, M. J., Pierce, J. L. and Laslett, B. (2008) *Telling Stories: The Use of Personal Narratives in the Social Sciences and History*. Ithaca, NY: Cornell University Press.

Modelski, T. (1991) *Feminism without Women: Culture & Criticism in a 'Postfeminist' Age*. New York, NY: Routledge.

Neville-Jan, A. (2004) Selling your soul to the devil: an auto-ethnography of pain, pleasure and the quest for a child. *Disability & Society* 19, 2: 113–27.

O'Brien, J. (2010) Seldom told tales from the field: guest editor's introduction to the special issue. *Journal of Contemporary Ethnography* 39: 471–82.

O'Byrne, P. (2007) The advantages and disadvantages of mixing methods: an analysis combining traditional and autoethnographic approaches, *Qualitative Health Research*, 17: 1381–91.

Nyong'o, T. (2013) Situating precarity between the body and the commons. *Women & Performance: A Journal of Feminist Theory* 23, 2: 157–61.

Pathak, A. A. (2010) Opening my voice, claiming my space: theorizing the possibilities of postcolonial approaches to autoethnography. *Journal of Research Practice* 6, 1: M10. Available at http://jrp.icaap.org/index.php/jrp/article/view/231/191 (accessed 31 March 2016).

Puar, J. (2012) Precarity talk: a virtual roundtable with Lauren Berlant, Judith Butler, Bojana Cvejic, Isabell Lorey, Jasbir Puar and Ana Vujanovic; edited by Jasbir Puar. *TDR: The Drama Review* 56, 4: 163–77.

Reed-Danahay, D. (1997a) *Auto/ethnography: Rewriting the Self and the Social*. Oxford: Berg.

Reed-Danahay, D. (1997b) 'Introduction'. In Reed-Danahay, D. (ed.), *Auto/Ethnography: Rewriting the Self and the Social*. Oxford: Berg, pp. 1–17.

Reinharz, S. (1992) *Feminist Methods in Social Research*. Oxford: Oxford University Press.

Richardson, L. (2000a) Evaluating ethnography. *Qualitative Inquiry* 6, 2: 253–5.

Richardson, L. (2000b) Introduction. Assessing alternative modes of qualitative and ethnographic research: how do we judge? Who judges? *Qualitative Inquiry* 6, 2: 251–2.

Richardson, L. (2000c) 'Writing: a method of inquiry'. In Denzin, N. K. and Lincoln, Y. S. (eds.), *Handbook of Qualitative Research*. Thousand Oaks: Sage Publications, pp. 923–49.

Richardson, L. (2003) Looking Jewish. *Qualitative Inquiry* 9, 5: 815–21.

Ronai, C. R. and Ellis, C. (1989) Turn-ons for money: interactional strategies of the table dancer. *Journal of Contemporary Ethnography* 18, 3: 271–98.

Sarachild, K. (1975) 'The power of history'. *Feminist Revolution*. New York, NY: Feminist Revolutions, pp. 7–29.

Sarachild, K. (1969) 'Appendix'. *Feminist Revolution*, New York, NY: Feminist Revolutions.

Shenin, D., Thompson, K., McDonald, S. N. and Clement, S. (2016) 'Betty Friedan to Beyoncé: today's generation embraces feminism on its own terms'. *Washington Post*, 27 January 2016.

Shomali, M. B. (2012) Storytelling: or, autoethnography in the academic industrial complex. *Feminist Wire*, 14 September, p. 47.

Short, N. P, Turner, L. and Grant, A. (2013) 'Introduction: storying life and lives'. In Grant, A., Short, N. P. and Turner, L. (eds.), *Contemporary British Autoethnography. Studies in Professional Life & Work, Vol. 9*. Rotterdam: Sense Publishers, pp. 1–16.

Smart, C. (2007) *Personal Life*. Cambridge: Polity Press.

Smith, C. (2005) Epistemological intimacy: a move to autoethnography. *International Journal of Qualitative Methods* 4, 2: 68–76.

Sotirin, P. (2010) Autoethnographic mother-writing: advocating radical specificity. *Journal of Research Practice* 6, 1: Article M9, 1–15.

Sparkes, A. (2003) 'Bodied, identities, selves: autoethnographic fragments and reflections'. In Denison, J. and Markula, P. (eds.), *Moving Writing: Crafting Writing in Sport Research*. New York, NY: Peter Lang, pp. 51–76.

Spry, T. (2001) Performing authoethnography: an embodied methodological praxis. *Qualitative Inquiry* 7, 6: 706–32.

Stacey, J. (1991) 'Can there be a feminist ethnography?'. In Gluck, S. B. and Patai, D. (eds.) *Women's Words: The Feminist Practice of Oral History*. New York, NY: Routledge, pp. 111–20.

Stanley, L. (1992) *The Auto/Biographical. I: The Theory and Practice of Feminist Auto/Biography*. Manchester, UK: Manchester University Press.

Stanley, L. (1993) On auto/biography in sociology. *Sociology* 27, 1: 41–52.

Stanley, L. (1994) 'The knowing because experiencing subject: narratives, lives and autobiography'. In Lennon, K. and Whitford, M. (eds.), *Knowing the Difference: Feminist Perspectives in Epistemology*. London, Routledge, pp. 132–48.

Tedlock, B. (2000) 'Ethnography and ethnographic representation'. In Denzin, N. K. and Lincoln, Y. S. (eds.), *Handbook of Qualitative Research*. Thousand Oaks, CA: Sage Publications. pp. 455–86.

Tomaselli, K. G., Dyll-Myklebust, L. and van Grootheest, S. (2013) 'Personal/political interventions via autoethnography: dualisms, knowledge, power, and performativity in research relations'. In Holman Jones, S., Adams, T. E. and Ellis, C. (eds.), *Handbook of Autoethnography*. Walnut Creek, CA: Left Coast Press, pp. 576–94.

Vannini, P. (2008) A queen's drowning: material culture, drama, and the performance of a technological accident. *Symbolic Interaction* 31, 2: 155–82.

Vidal-Ortiz, S. (2004) On being a white person of color: using autoethnography to understand Puerto Ricans' racialization. *Qualitative Sociology* 27, 2: 179–203.

Wolcott, H. F. (2004) The ethnographic autobiography. *Auto/Biography* 12, 2: 93–106.

1 Being a 'sexual pervert' in academia

I wanted to move out of the flat world of most sociological accounts of relationships . . . incorporate the kinds of emotional and relational dimensions that are meaningful in everyday life . . . it was no longer appropriate to reflect upon 'other people' as if being a sociologist entitled one to be apart from these cultural shifts, emotional tides and personal feelings.

(Smart, 2007: 3–4)

Introduction

This chapter is a good example of how as a lesbian feminist scholar, I tackled the structural constraints and career diversions that many LGBTQI scholars confronted over the past four decades. Using autoethnography as a feminist method, I begin this chapter by recounting my journey as a Catholic nun (and closeted lesbian) through social and community activism of the late 1960s to early 1970s in East Coast, US. I also provide a glimpse of what it was like to be involved in feminist sociology at the London School of Economics (LSE), University of London in the 1970s and the influence of British and American feminism on my postgraduate research on lesbians. I then turn my attention to the impact of drugs and alcohol research on my lesbian feminist sociological imagination and vice versa. Lastly, I reflect upon my contributions to the sociology of the body and the construction of deviant bodies' within a genetics moral order. All of what I say is framed by my being a feminist sociologist in academia since the 1970s. I hope to show how being in this situation feels and how as a result of my life changing, precarious experiences, I was propelled into political life. This chapter emerges from the growing body of work by LGBTQI scholars (Adams, 2011; Adams and Holman Jones, 2011; Berry, 2006; Crawley, 2002, 2008; Eguchi, 2015; Gust, 2007; Joshi, 2007; Macdonald, 2013; Munoz, 1995; Philareatou and Allen, 2006; Trotter *et al.*, 2006; Vannini, 2008) who reflect autoethnographically upon their positions *vis-à-vis* heteronormativity, albeit this work may be viewed as marginal in relation to conventional academic canons (Plummer, 2009). Nevertheless, I introduce autoethnography as a methodological tool for speaking and writing reflexively about being out in academia and developing a 'critical sexology' (Barker, 2006). Similar to other academics, whether sociologists (Glassner and Hertz, 2003), women (Krieger, 1996), lesbian couples

(Gibson and Meem, 2006) or lesbian and gay scholars (McNaron, 1996), I want my story to resonate.

My story begins . . .

18 June 1966

It is a beautiful sunny day in Bridgeport, Connecticut and I can smell the cherry blossoms in the clear air as I sit in our back yard and ponder my future life. I feel so happy to graduate from high school. I do well in my studies but unlike most, if not all of my friends, I am not going to a large college or university. I look forward in August to entering the convent of the Sisters of Mercy in my home state, Connecticut, where I will be studying at a very small Catholic girls' college, St Joseph's College. My college training includes university-level courses (much to the relief of my dad), but in my first three years of training, these course will be focused mainly on theology and philosophy. I will soon be a postulant and start my preparation to be a fully fledged nun with final vows of poverty, chastity and obedience in six years.

20 June 1966

Unbeknown to me, my friends are giving me a surprise party at my house. My parents are complicit. I park the car in the driveway as I arrive home from the grocery store. I open the back door, 'Surprise!' I hear my friends and parents yell. I am astonished and almost drop my bag of groceries as I go into the living room. My mother hurries to take the bag away from me, looks at me with a big smile and squeezes my hand as she relieves me of the grocery bag. I am still astonished. Immediately, my friend Betsy says, 'It's about time, Sister Betsy. We've been waiting a long time'. I laugh and say, 'How did you plan this? I never knew'. Maureen chirps in, 'You weren't meant to. We just wanted a get together before you are locked in the nunnery forever'. Everyone laughs.

25 August 1966

It is my entrance day to the Sisters of Mercy. My family drive me to the Sisters of Mercy novitiate in Madison, Connecticut. It is a beautiful August day and the novitiate is by the sea. As we enter the grounds, I can already smell the salty sea air. I look out the car window and see that a few of my high school friends have come to say goodbye to me. I am excited to enter the convent. It feels like I have waited many years to fulfil my promise to God. I wear my postulant habit with pride and my trunk with all of my other personal things have been delivered to the novitiate the week before. For the past two years, I have had a deep sense that I have a vocation – that God is calling me to serve him in this world. But still, I am anxious because I have had, for many years, secret attractions to women. I have not acted on these attractions but they have been strong, especially in my Senior year in high school. I think, 'At least, I don't have to date men anymore. No, I will be surrounded by women who I desire'. Deep in my heart, I know I won't dare to act on my desires or lesbian feelings. 'Or won't I?', I ask myself fearful of my answer. My father stops the car and I open the door and step out. I am excited and afraid at the same time.

3 May 1970

I am in West Hartford, Connecticut at the Motherhouse, the main centre where Mother Superior, the head of my religious order, lives. I asked to leave the convent two months ago. I have already been in the convent for nearly four years. I took temporary vows of poverty, chastity and obedience last summer but it has been hard going for me. I feel that I do not belong and I am full of fear for my future. So I tell my sisters that I want to leave the novitiate. I do not feel like I have a vocation. At that time, I write to the Pope to ask if I can live outside the convent until my temporary vows expire, so to speak. If he agrees, then soon I will be exclaustrated.[1] I learn from my Mother Superior that the response from the Pope has been received this week and I am free to leave the convent, but I am required to report to the Motherhouse in West Hartford, Connecticut. There my Mother will be waiting for me to take me home. I sit in the waiting room next to Mother Superior's office. I hear my mother's voice. She is talking to Mother Superior. I hear her say, 'We must go now, where is Betsy?'. Her voice is loud. She sounds irritated. I could tell she is upset. The door opens and my mother appears. She looks somewhat shaken and without hugging me, she grabs my hand and says immediately, 'Betsy, let's go and get out of here'. No one is around as we leave. This feels strange to me. My mother walks quickly, still holding my hand and I have a hard time keeping up with her. As we leave the building, she says with an exasperated voice, 'I have never been so insulted in my life'. I ask, 'Why? What happened?'. My mother says, 'Keep walking, Betsy. I'll tell you in the car'. When we get in the car, she scurries in, starts up and waits for me to fasten my seat belt. She is silent and looks cross. She drives off quickly from the parking lot, turns right on the main road and begins with a huge sigh of relief, 'I am so happy you left that place. You don't belong there, Betsy. I know you still have two years of your temporary vows left. But, you are too good for them'. Astonished, I ask, 'Why? Why would you say that, Mom?'. 'Can you imagine', she continues now with a raised voice, 'That Mother Superior whatever her name is tried to suggest that you are mentally ill and that is the reason you are leaving the convent. Well, I won't have any of that nonsense. They are the sick ones, as far as I am concerned'. I feel as if I am betrayed deeply. 'What', I think 'How can she say that? I was only unhappy'. I am speechless for a few seconds and say to my mother, 'Why would Mother Superior say that about me? I just felt recently that I don't have a vocation, God hasn't called me and I was not happy to have my life always dictated by others – obedience was the killer, Mom'. Quickly, Mom responds, 'Well, I am glad to hear that and you're not mentally ill and her comments are ridiculous. Maybe, they say that about all the girls who leave or become exclaustrated. By the way, there's a packet of cigarettes in the glove compartment. Help yourself'. 'Thanks, Mom, you're an angel and thanks for coming to pick me up'. I open the window, light up the cigarette, inhale and look out at the Connecticut countryside. 'What a relief', I think, 'I am out of that place', but I still *feel hurt at what Mother Superior said to my mother. As I look out, I wonder, 'What will the future hold?'.*

12 August 1970

A letter addressed to me arrives home from Fordham University, a Catholic Jesuit University in the Bronx Borough of New York City. I open it and read it. It says, 'We are writing to inform you that you are accepted as a transfer student to Fordham University, Thomas More College. We have accepted all of your credits from St Joseph's College. You will be enrolled as a Junior year undergraduate'. I think, Fantastic! Immediately, feeling elated, I put down the letter and run to tell my mother.

Catholic elitism creates a political sociologist

4 February 1971

The sun is shining, but it is freezing. I am standing outside Dealy Hall at Fordham University. I love being here and am an extremely ebullient student. I ponder, 'No one knows that I am a Catholic nun who completed a two-year novitiate, including a year of silence . . . I dedicated my life to vows of poverty, chastity and obedience . . . I am having my first lesbian affair with sweet Sharon, another nun. I am rather anxious and have no habit on. I am in 'civis' as we nuns call our 'lay clothes'. I am a transfer student from St Joseph's College but no one knows why. As a nun who left my community, the Sisters of Mercy, I have a visceral sense of relief that I don't need to worry about my vows. I study sociology, a new subject to me. My heart races as I think about Sharon. I am in love but uncomfortable in the knowledge that she is in Connecticut being a real nun. I ask myself, 'Am I a lesbian?'. Without answering, I push this guilty secret deep inside me and carry on with my student life. I feel so guilt ridden that a week later I develop non-specific uticaria (i.e. hives all over my body) which my doctor announces as 'stress related'.

Before I left the convent, I was active in the anti-war movement. I knew Fordham would be a good place to continue my political activity. In Catholic terms, Fordham, as a Jesuit institution, was a hotbed of social protest with an active branch of Students for a Democratic Society (SDS). Much to the dismay of the FBI, Fordham provided political sanctuary for the peace activist and poet Daniel Berrigan, a Jesuit priest and member of Catonsville nine who doused military draft files with napalm and set them ablaze. Also, I knew in terms of my intellectual development, I would be able to build upon my scholastic training which I had during my convent years. 'Maybe I'd even fantasize less about Sharon and feel less guilty', I contemplate.

I'm at Dealy Hall because I'm dropping off a book from one of my lecturers. Dealy is a large brick building that houses the Department of Sociology and Anthropology. I've become accustomed to it during the past five months. I see Professor Fitzpatrick exit Dealy. 'Fitz', as he is known, is a Jesuit priest, the chair and founder of the

Department of Sociology and Anthropology the first such department created in a Catholic college in the US. Last semester, I took his Introduction to Sociology course. I really enjoyed it, and the examples drawn from his experience as a political activist and scholar. As Fitz sees me, he says, 'Hi Betsy, I liked your Intro essay last semester; it was excellent'. He smiled, turned away and rushed on. Feeling overwhelmed by excitement, I shout after to him, 'Thanks, Fitz'. I almost burst into tears and muse elatedly to myself, 'Gosh . . . Fitz has a reputation of being a hard marker. How did I do it?' Two weeks later, I learn that I get an A on Fitz's course. This knowledge spurs me on to take his other undergraduate courses, SOC 193 Community and SOC 177 Social Change in Latin America. I sense Fordham is a breath of fresh air and I am happy here.

Social justice: becoming a political sociologist

In his article, 'Catholic and Evangelical elites in dialogue and alliance', Rutan (1995) discusses Catholic elites. Fitz is mentioned as one who endorsed Rutan's paper. Whether or not Fitz would have seen himself as a 'Catholic elite' is an interesting question. Fitz studied with Talcott Parsons at Harvard University and he often mentioned Parson's work, specifically the idea that social conflict is functional in society. Fitz would probably have seen himself as a 'strategic or structural/functional elite whose ethical imperatives of good and religious duty and obligations offer no less tangible rewards than power, wealth, achievement and fame for non-religious elites' (Rutan, 1995: 114). Regardless of whether or not Fitz saw himself as an elite of moral, religious, philosophical and educational pre-eminence, he was a sociologist of his time[2] and a political voice calling attention to the challenges of an expanding Hispanic population in the US and the social injustices they experienced.

Fitz was active in Ivan Illich's Centre for Intercultural Documentation in Cuernavaca, Mexico. He worked with Illich and others such as Paulo Freire and Peter Berger of 'The Social Construction of Reality' fame. There Fitz developed his passion for social justice. Fitz's studies ranged from issues of education to the problems of juvenile delinquency and intervention. He was before his time and called for a national immigration policy to support the quintessentially American experience of allowing access to opportunity. In class, we asked questions such as 'why do Americans discriminate against Puerto Ricans?', 'what does poverty in inner cities mean in "melting pot" America?', 'what does social justice mean for contemporary sociologists?' and 'why are Americans prejudiced?'. Discussions in Fitz's classes were always politically orientated and my university experience was steeped in the pastoral challenges of a changing, politicized Catholic church.

18 March 1972

I find myself meditating – reflecting on my life in my post-convent days, as I call it now. I find it soothing in my now somewhat hectic life as a student. I tell myself, 'All of this is new and exciting, but I can never tell anyone about my lesbianism.

How strange to use this word, lesbianism. I grew up in a religious family of second-generation European immigrants (i.e. Hungarians, Romanians and Italians). My background 'helps' on the religious fervour front but not the lesbianism front. There must be hope because I am more interested in sociology than my religion. I've got to gain more courage to explore my lesbianism'.

May 1972

I am a research assistant for Jim Brown a sociologist at Fordham. One day, I say, 'Jim, I am having an affair with a woman'. Jim says casually, 'Betsy maybe you are a lesbian'. I feel an acute sense of shock, but perceive that he does not see me any different from anyone else. I say, 'OK, Jim, but please don't tell anyone'. Later, Jim asks me to do a tutorial on 'sexual deviance' as well as work on a comparative project on drug use amongst American College students with the criminologist Daniel Glazer from the University of Southern California. During this time, Jim introduces me to the sociologist John Gagnon when we visit a drug clinic in Manhattan. I am excited by Gagnon's ideas on 'sexual scripts' which, unbeknownst to me at the time, I would explore in my PhD studies. By June 1972, when I graduated from Fordham University, I left the convent and began to focus my intellectual energies on 'doing sociology'. Although I told Jim about Sharon, I deny being a lesbian because 'Anyhow, Sharon and I split up in June and she is planning to marry an ex-priest'. I become engaged to John, a student I meet at Fordham. At least 'I love him', I think to myself.

September 1972

As I wave goodbye to my mother at JFK airport, I say, 'Take care of yourself'. She is crying. I feel somewhat lost and confused. I have a sense that I am free to be myself – but feel unsure of what that means about my lesbian feelings. I smile at John and as we take off for London, I murmur, 'Goodbye, Big Apple'.

The 'marriage of convenience' between deviance theory and lesbian feminist sociology

The next few years in England have their ups and downs. There is not enough space here to explore what transpires. Nevertheless, I feel my sexuality, my identity, my embodied core is shifting: I marry, I divorce, I leave the Church, I come out as a lesbian and I embark on the first sociology PhD on lesbians in the UK. In October 1973, I am a postgraduate student at LSE. The intellectual atmosphere is buzzing. I am in David Downe's and Paul Rock's thought-provoking seminar, 'Criminology and deviancy theory', which meets every Thursday. I have many student colleagues studying with me who will become well-known sociologists. Although enjoying deviance theory, I am interested in feminist sociology, which is developing at a fast rate both in the UK and US. I sense that feminist sociology will help me figure out some of the pressing theoretical issues that relate to my research, especially my ideas on lesbian identity, female sexuality, lesbian social organisation, reproduction and labour power – key concepts for my PhD entitled 'The sociology of lesbianism: female 'deviance' and female sexuality'.

October 1973

My supervisor, Professor Terry Morris meets with me every three months (much to the envy of my other student colleagues who see their supervisors once a year). Terry encourages me with stories of his own PhD study of juvenile delinquency awarded in 1955 and published subsequently in 1957 (The Criminal Area: A Study in Social Ecology). *Terry loves talking about his observational work and is very inspiring. He gives me hints about good ethnographic practice, 'Betsy, why don't you do observational work on lesbians in London. I am sure it will be fruitful and you will learn how to become a good, empirical sociologist. The key is to watch and listen'. I say, 'OK, Terry. It is a big challenge but I am up for it!'. I begin my study of the London lesbian community and use the Festival Inn as one of my key ethnographic sites. It has a mixed reputation among lesbians and gays.[3]*

I meet Hilary Rose and Jalna Hanmer at LSE and attend Hilary's lectures. This is before their classic paper is published, 'Women's liberation, reproduction, and the technological fix' from the 1974 BSA Conference on 'Sexual Divisions and Society' (Rose and Hanmer, 1976). Their paper asks how far reproductive technologies oppress rather than liberate women. I am excited and intrigued by what I am learning about women's oppression. 'Am I becoming a feminist?', I continually ask myself. I read Simone de Beauvoir's, The Second Sex. *I hear Germaine Greer talk at Bedford College on her book,* The Female Eunuch. *I take a month preparing a lecture on 'Sexism in the Founding Fathers of Sociology' for our weekly informally organised postgraduate seminars on Women's Rights at LSE. Being a good ethnographer, I attend the first National Lesbian Conference in Bristol and collect data for my PhD. I also march on my first women's march with the Socialist Workers Party. While walking all the way to Parliament, we chant feminist slogans and my voice gets hoarse. I tell Mary, my Socialist Workers Party (SWP) friend, 'I hope we don't get arrested because if I do, the authorities will deport me as an American'. I submit my PhD in December 1977 and have my* viva *in April 1978 with Keith Soothill, my external examiner. I am exhausted while at the same time exhilarated at my accomplishments.*

I am unable to convey here all of the theoretical as well as personal and emotional changes involved from being a political sociologist to becoming a feminist sociologist during this time. In terms of my theoretical developments in *Lesbians, Women and Society* (Ettorre, 1980), the published version of my PhD, my aim is to make lesbianism visible as a public and political issue in sociology. I see this as a reflection of how I live my own life. Along with many feminists writing on sex, gender, family, violence and rape, I want to show that these issues, including lesbianism, are all seemingly private and personal matters but are in fact public, political issues. I want to broach the public–private distinctions on lesbianism and take a step towards a social theory of lesbianism.

One reviewer (Stoneall, 1981: 572–3) aptly states:

> Ettorre is very good on the political aspect and on the stages and preconditions of becoming political. Ettorre's empirical study is cradled between theoretical chapters that relate lesbianism to patriarchy and capitalism. Lesbians defy the traditional sexual division of labour. Lesbians seek economic independence from men, and they also threaten dominant sexual ideology . . . On the other hand, Ettorre does not sacrifice the complexities of lesbian experiences to sweeping generalities. She shows the range and variety of lesbian life – from in to out of the closet, from monogamy to affairs to friendships to ghettoes, from straight to conformist to reformist to radical, from having children to not, from varied relationships with men, from bisexual to celibate . . . She . . . show [s] the contradictions . . . between capitalism and patriarchy . . . [–] the dialectics of power. . . . Ettorre shows the necessity of fighting both [Marxist and Radical feminism] and obliterating dichotomies within sexuality, gender, and labour to eliminate power . . . Ettorre's theoretical and empirical study fills a void in sociology. Few books on gender devote more than a page to lesbianism, and studies of lesbians are rare. One hopes for a further development of her theory.

As fate would have it, Stoneall's hope (and mine) will never be fulfilled.

Patriarchy, dependence and the hierarchy of drugs

December 1978

Terry phones me . . . quite excited, he says, 'Betsy, have you seen the job advertised at the Addiction Research Unit (ARU), Institute of Psychiatry. You must apply for it. They are looking for a Research Sociologist and it's just for you'. 'Are they looking for someone to do research on lesbians?' I ask. 'No', he replies, 'they want someone familiar with deviance theory and I am sure you have a chance of getting it'. Terry is acutely aware that since getting my PhD I have been applying steadily for academic posts with no luck. I am depressed. He also knows that doing a sociology PhD on lesbians is not attracting future employers' interest. He continues, 'Betsy, you're going to have to emphasize your knowledge of deviance theory and I'll give you a good reference. At least, it's a step up on the ladder'. 'OK, Terry, I'll apply', I say, feeling anxious.

I am offered the post and stay at the ARU for seven years. It is an important time in my intellectual development. I work on a number of interesting projects in the drugs and alcohol field. However, it is not easy, because I make the decision to be totally out as a lesbian. As a result, weekly if not daily, I am the brunt of gay jokes and insults.[4]

January 1979

I arrive at work after being hurt by an air gun shot by someone hiding near where I live. A secretary asks, 'Why do you have a bandage on your temple?' 'Oh, someone shot me on Lupus Street', I reply hesitantly 'and I went to my doctor who put it there'. A psychiatrist colleague in the office turns towards me and says with derision, 'What do you expect writing a book about perverts'. I walk out of the office hurt and disgusted, feeling as if I am kicked in my heart. I go quietly back to my office, sobbing and ensure that my door is locked.

December 1979

I learn that everyday at work if I am alone in the common room and a particular male colleague sees me, he makes an excuse to talk to me and grabs my backside. This happens almost every day and it annoys me. I say nothing because I don't know that what he is doing is sexual harassment. I only discover that it is when I tell a group of feminist friends at a consciousness raising session. They are astonished, tell me it's not my fault and if I don't want to bring a complaint against him – at least slap his hand hard. Next time, I do and I know I hurt his hand as it caught my rings. Nevertheless, the harassment continues for years until I leave the ARU.

March 1980

My position at the ARU is not enhanced when a journalist claiming to be from *The Guardian* but is from the *News of the World* publishes a controversial piece on my work. It is rather unfortunate that the piece comes out on the same day as the London Women's Research and Resources Centre's sponsored conference, 'Women's Liberation and Men'. My friends buy frantically all of the *News of the World* newspapers within a half mile radius of the conference venue. They say they do not want me to 'get caught'. Of course, I am aware that it is not 'politically correct' for lesbian feminists to publish in *News of the World* and, given that I am due to talk at this conference (see Ettorre, 1982), we all want to stave off any negative reactions from participants who will not know that I made a mistake by agreeing to be interviewed before asking for press identification.

April 1980

Working on a national study of alcohol treatment units, I interview a consultant psychiatrist who says, 'I don't allow any violent men to become patients but, if they beat their wives, it is not proper violence. I'll admit them'. Inwardly, I am horrified and think, 'A real misogynist'. I feel my lesbian feminist sensibilities are heightened and I become enraged at such antipathy towards women.

This time in my career is less than easy because my identity politics leads to my personal life, work and activism becoming 'sites of political expression' (Taylor and

Raeburn, 1995: 254). My experience generates a deep passion. I use my anger to write about women and substance use and to continue to be totally out.

June 1980

I reflect, 'I have an excellent opportunity to make a visible contribution to a field which has been resistant both theoretically and methodologically to an approach sensitive to the needs of women. I must press on'.

Gradually, I start to write about women and substance use in my spare time and on weekends. A high point is when Carol Smart joins the ARU. For a brief period of time, I have a real feminist mate.[5]

In March 1984, Susanne MacGregor invites me to Birkbeck College to take up a Senior Researcher post on an evaluation of the Central Funding Initiative (CFI; see MacGregor *et al.*, 1990). This work demonstrates that the government's support of statutory and non-statutory drug services is crucial given the mounting visibility of HIV/AIDS. I know already of the impact of HIV/AIDs on the gay community from my gay male friends. Birkbeck is a turning point because it enables me to work in a supportive, intellectual environment, open to me as an 'out lesbian'. Not only did I have the pleasure of working closely with Susanne MacGregor, but I also had inspiring intellectual discussions with Paul Hirst, Sami Zabida, Ben Pimlott, Arthur Lipow, John Solomos, Ross Coomber, Tim Rhodes, Richard Hartnoll, Harriet Lodge, Bernard Crick and Janet Holland.

August 1984

Jo Campling phones me. 'Betsy I want you to do a book on women and substance use in my Women in Society series'. I respond excitedly, 'How fantastic, I would love to Jo, the experiences of women substance users need to be recognised and valued and someone needs to create a critical framework in which the production of feminist knowledge becomes a possibility'.

Gradually, I find that by centring on men – the most socially 'visible' participants within drug-using cultures – 'scientific' research in the addiction field tends to uphold traditional 'patriarchal' images of men and women. As a result, a distorted view of women is presented. I develop two key conceptions which, unbeknownst to me at the time, endure throughout my career: dependence and a hierarchy of drugs. Both are key to my professional development given I am determined as a feminist academic (1) not to be dependent upon the patriarchal ideas and patronage that exist in the alcohol and drug field and (2) to demonstrate that a hierarchy of drugs linked with moralities about what 'deviant bodies' are and are not acceptable exists. Indeed, I experienced being unacceptable or 'perverted' at the ARU and I want to explore how the territorialisation of my own 'deviance' relates to 'deviant bodies' using drugs.

I apply these ideas in *Women and Substance Use* (Ettorre, 1992) and *Women and Alcohol: From a Private Pleasure to a Public Problem?* (Ettorre, 1997). In the latter, I develop the concepts of negative and positive drinking and demonstrate how pleasure is a taboo subject in the addiction field. In this early and later work (Ettorre, 2007), I use this notion of dependence and link it to the related notion of hierarchy of drugs and, in turn, pollution. In later work with Nancy Campbell (Campbell and Ettorre, 2011) I use the notion of epistemologies of ignorance[6] to demonstrate how strategies of knowing, as well as not knowing, are embedded in the drugs and alcohol field. All my ideas emerge from my thinking as a lesbian working in this field and I gradually find that boundaries between 'deviant bodies' are able to break down. Although I am acutely aware that I am not able to develop further my earlier theories on lesbianism, I do have the pleasure of editing *Making Lesbians Visible in the Substance Use Field* (Ettorre, 2005a), which enables a group of young lesbian researchers to publish. As I say in the Introduction to this book:

> In looking specifically at lesbian substance users, we need to choose intentionally how we will transform obsolete ideas, beliefs and practices as we construct 'lesbian sensitive' perspectives . . . this volume is an important step in helping to create an environment in which the hurt of invisibility of lesbian substance users can begin to be healed.
>
> (Ettorre, 2005b, 4–5)

My career as a contract researcher changes when in 1991 I leave the UK and move to Helsinki, Finland. I want to be with my life partner, Imma. I realise that being an openly lesbian academic in Finland is not *de rigueur* as many Finnish lesbian and gay academics remain in the closet. I do not. The well-known Finnish medical sociologist Elianne Riska invites me to do an Academy of Finland-funded study on tranquilliser use. Our study is published eventually as *Gendered Moods: Psychotropics and Society* (Ettorre and Riska, 1995) and reveals clear gendered reasons for psychotropic drug use in Finland.

When we finish this study, I want to continue my earlier work on gender and illegal drugs; however, it is very difficult to do any research on illegal drugs in Finland. This is because the main focus is on alcohol, which is seen as an indigenous drug. Illegal drugs, such as heroin or cocaine, are seen as 'foreign substances' (i.e. imported from abroad) and perceived as much more threatening than, for example, Koskenkorva (Finnish national vodka).

February 1993

One day I meet a well-known Finnish researcher and say, 'Matti, I would like to do research on illegal drugs'. Displaying an irritated manner and making a face, Matti says, 'Betsy, we don't have illegal drug users in Finland'. Then remembering the dirty needles I see on the street where I live, I say casually, 'Oh well, I guess you must have poor diabetics'. I think, 'Being an out lesbian won't enhance my chances of getting research contracts'. And it doesn't.

Genetic capital, gendered bodies and reproductive asceticism

October 1996

I sit in the hospital office of a well-known obstetrician in a European city. He is . . . late for our scheduled interview . . . I feel anxious because I have a series of questions I want to ask him. As we discuss, I find his views on ethics quite maverick – you could say distorted. At one point, he says, 'We make up our own ethics as we go along'. I try not to look astonished and continue with the interview which he (not me) is in control of. He continues, 'If a patient does not agree to an abortion before we perform an amniocentesis I won't carry out the procedure. We don't want any more disabled people in this country . . . I think to myself shuttering, 'I bet if he could, he would make sure all future LGBTQI foetuses are aborted!'.

While living in Finland, I develop an interest in the sociology of the new genetics – an interest spurned on by a gnawing sense over the years that many people think being 'queer' is genetic. I never do and thus want to explore this relatively new area in sociology – not related to sexualities *per se* but a different field – reproduction. I put together a proposal on genetics and prenatal screening with some European colleagues. Genetics was beginning to make headlines but the Human Genome Project had yet to be completed. Surprisingly, we receive European Commission funding. I am the project coordinator and eventually we publish the results (Ettorre, 2001). My main focus during this research is to mount a comparative study of genetic experts. My earlier story relates to my visit to one expert. Often, I come across these sorts of ideas and I decide to write a book in which the voices of experts are heard alongside those of pregnant women (Ettorre, 2002).

I observe that pregnant bodies who undergo invasive prenatal tests are disciplining themselves. I call this form of self-disciplining 'reproductive asceticism' and see it as a form of self-surveillance, necessary for the regulation of 'fit' populations in our consumer culture. I write about how the female body emerges as a reproductive resource – a corporeal asset through which any woman is able to assume an indelible moral identity. Before I move back to England in March 1998 to take up a Readership at the University of Plymouth, I begin explorations into the sociology of the body. I am influenced by Bourdieu's (1984) work on how the body in contemporary culture is a comprehensive form of physical capital – a possessor of power, status and distinction, integral to the accumulation of cultural and social resources. Of course, I continually experience my own 'distinction' and how my 'lesbian body' has less status and cultural capital in both academia and society.

Whether or not a pregnant woman has social worth in reproduction, 'good genes' or valuable genetic capital, she is bound by a genetic moral order. I see this as an unintended consequence of reproductive genetics: the creation of divisions between good reproducing bodies and bad reproducing bodies. Basically, women are separated into good or bad reproducers.

May 1997

Doing my genetics research, I often think with sadness of the experiences of my 82-year-old mother and other mothers of LGBTQI individuals. I ask myself, 'Were they perceived as bad reproducing bodies?'. 'Probably', I answer without hesitation.

Embedded in twenty-first century science and rationality are gendered, classed, racialized and heterosexist notions of nature and the belief that normality and abnormality are heritable (Steinberg, 1997: 67).[7] Through these powerful practices, individualized mechanistic bodies are privileged because 'experts' remain averse to dealing with sentient bodies: the body as a machine prevails. A process of 'embodied deviance', the scientific and lay claim that bodies of individuals classified as deviant are marked in some recognizable way exists (Urla and Terry 1995: 2). 'Deviant' social behaviour, including LGBTQI behaviour, consistently manifests itself in the substance of the 'deviant's' (i.e. LGBTQI's) body. These bodies are seen to deviate from heteronormativity and perceived as socially and morally inferior. Our social and moral trouble making is embodied because we are constituted as a 'menace' in society (Inness, 1997: 5). Regardless of the fact that throughout my academic career my 'deviance' is embodied or appears as menacing, I find creative 'technologies of the self' (Foucault, 1984) to engage in.

March 1999

I ask myself, 'What particular disciplinary practices besides being categorised as "lesbian", "deviant" or "menacing" are available to me as a lesbian academic? How do I address my continually emerging lesbianism as I engage in different fields of study? What technologies of self are at work in my desire to be an accomplished academic while an out lesbian? Why do I have a deep desire for other LGBTQI scholars to privilege my story over those we see twenty-five times a day? Was I too early for sociology?'

In my autoethnography, I construct and engage in a number of technologies or embodied practices that are fulfilling to me. I go to a Catholic University. I stay in the closet. I have a relationship with a nun. I move to England. I come out. I do a PhD on lesbianism. I accept I am not marketable as a lesbian researcher. I develop feminist ideas in different areas of research. I move to Finland. I accept that being a lesbian academic may have its ups and downs. I am the target of jokes. I am insulted and in pain. Although difficult, I learn not to regret what I have chosen. I do all of these practices in order to learn how to be more reflexive as a lesbian. They 'work'.

December 2007

I ponder to myself, 'I do not plan on feeling proud. This must be an added extra'.

These various technologies of my lesbian self remind me that I am deeply embodied. Because I am deeply embodied, I am also profoundly dissatisfied with the dominant Cartesian paradigm of rationality that ruptures mind and body at the heart of Western society. This dominant paradigm shapes, as well as typifies, acceptable body images of a 'lesbian feminist academic' for both the minority and majority cultures to which I belong. My story needs to be a direct challenge to my 'embodied deviance' as well as a movement away from the notion that a single cultural perspective on being a lesbian academic exists within the lesbian, academic and sociological community.

February 2008

I feel excited and nervous. Too warm and sweating slightly in my academic robe, I adjust my hood and look at the audience as I walk to the podium. Some are smiling. Feeling thrilled, I notice someone left flowers on the podium. I look up with a sense of pride and begin with a strong voice, 'I want my inaugural lecture to begin on a personal note . . .'

This is a recollection of my inaugural lecture when I shared reflections on what it has meant to be a lesbian feminist sociologist in academia. In the lecture, I used the method of autoethnography. Colleagues asked me to publish this lecture.[8] I include some of this article in this chapter because I feel it is an excellent example of feminist autoethnography.[9]

November 2009

If someone asks, 'Where are you going now, Betsy?' I answer, 'I am searching for a politically grounded feminist sociology of the body which looks at how selected gendered, raced, disabled and sexualised bodies are consistently excluded from moral agency'.

August 2010

I am appointed head of my department. I do not want to do it because I am in the midst of doing a lot of writing. But my Dean points out to me that in my contract it states that I have to do it if no one comes forward and no one does. So I am HoD. I hate being Head. I find it a difficult time because unfortunately I am shunned by most if not all of my colleagues. Although I never tell them, I suspect somehow they know that the Deputy Vice-Chncellor wants me to consider getting rid of what he calls, the 'unproductive' ones. I am sent to Coventry, so to speak.[10] *For me, this is a very unpleasant experience because I don't want to fire any of my colleagues. Immediately, I think about retiring.*

November 2010

One evening, my partner says, 'Listen Betsy, you are miserable and you are going to get sick. Why don't you retire? No one at the University will thank you as HoD and you are killing yourself with stress'. I am confused but I seriously consider what Imma says and the next week I arrange a meeting with the University personnel and ask to see what sort of retirement package they will offer me. I am slightly anxious but know I need to consider leaving the academy. I am a physical wreck – having headaches all of the time and generally stressed out. I receive papers that outline my disengagement deal and they are acceptable to me. I am starting to feel less confused. The administration says I can leave on 31 January 2011. I decide to take the plunge and feel immediately relieved.

January 2011

I am on a plane from London to Helsinki. 'Gosh what a relief', I say to myself. After being in the academy since the 1970s, I can now focus on myself and my own work. As the plane lands in Helsinki, I feel my stress leaving me. I am excited to see my partner Imma. I decide that I will take a break from academia for a few months and it ends up being a year.

September 2012

I decide to write a research application on autoethnography for an Emeritus Fellowship at the Leverhulme Trust in London. I am still resident in UK until we sell our house in Truro, Cornwall. I get the application in on time and wait. Excitedly, I think, 'Now I am ready to get back to work'.

A surprise email

25 April 2013

I am in Helsinki and just came home from a short run. I switch on my computer to check my email inbox. As my eyes scan what emails have arrived, I notice an email from the Leverhulme Trust. I quickly sit down and read it. It says:

> Dear Professor Ettorre,
>
> I am pleased to inform you that your grant application 'Writing the Self, the Other and the Social: Using Autoethnography as a Feminist Method of Sensitising the "I"' has been approved by the Leverhulme Trust. A detailed offer letter confirming the amount awarded will follow in the next week to 10 days, however we wished to send you the good news at once (you do not need to reply to this email) . . .
>
> Yours sincerely, The Leverhulme Trust.

While reading this email, I am totally astonished. Gradually, I feel excited and somewhat overwhelmed. Wow! I can't believe it. I am one of 36 scholars in the UK to receive this prestigious fellowship. This is wonderful. I sit back in my chair and look out the window.

I must take a shower. But before I do, I am remembering the days when I wrote the proposal. I recollect saying to myself, 'Don't hold back on being a feminist. Put the word feminist in the title'.

I did. And now this. What good luck! Now that I am retired and have no boss, I can do what I want. This work will give me a good opportunity to have fun, travel and to see some good friends and new contacts, particularly across the pond. Before taking a shower, I click on my now-successful proposal and start to read it out loud to myself: autoethnography lies firmly within the realm of postmodern (critical theory) ethnography (O'Byrne 2007), while being a study of culture that involves the self, . . . autoethnography symbolizes a postmodernist . . . intervention . . . autoethnography is an ideal method to study the 'feminist I' . . . I stop reading and look out the window and think, I want to really focus on autoethnography as a feminist method.

December 2014 – March 2015

I have a wonderful experience on my travels during my Fellowship.[11] I met with many friends and colleagues and discuss how autoethnography is a feminist method. I am particularly happy to meet so many graduate students who are interested in and doing autoethnography. I think, what a big change from my early years in the academy. There is no harassment, no bad jokes, no one telling me I am perverse, etc. – only sheer joy – the joy of sharing intellectual ideas . . .

June 2016

I feel a sense of relief when pondering these stories and my ideas, 'Perhaps, this is why my story is important'.

In conclusion, I want to give you, the reader, an idea of my journey as a lesbian feminist sociologist since the 1970s. Although, for some colleagues, my earlier work on lesbianism may (or may not) have been ground-breaking, I had to abandon it for my ultimate survival in the academic world. Nevertheless, being an out lesbian sustains me in my academic work and provides me with the intellectual armamentarium to survive in fields of thought beyond sexualities. Doing autoethnography has been a challenging way for me to reflect on my life, sensitise my feminist 'I' and to see why and how my embodied emotionality is important to share with others.

Notes

1 Officially, exclaustration means living outside the convent under vows and not having to have a Mother Superior to tell me what to do.
2 See www.fordham.edu/images/Whats_New/magazine/winter05/FordhamW_05_main18_19.pdf, accessed 5 February 2008.

3 In 2008, when I was preparing for my inaugural lecture, Ken Plummer reminded me that when I was doing my ethnographic work we both were thrown out of the Festival Inn in South London for leafleting information about Gay Liberation Front.
4 *As I write, I recollect, 'This was 1978 – Harvey Milk has just been assassinated'.*
5 It is emblematic how far we have come in the 30 years since I worked at the ARU that in March 2008, a month after my inaugural lecture at the University of Liverpool, the University College Union celebrated the LGBT history month for the first time.
6 We borrow the notion 'epistemologies of ignorance' from Tuana (2004, 2006) who contends that the women's health movement as a resistance movement was concerned with both the circulation of knowledge and ignorance: 'to fully understand the complex practices of knowledge production and the variety of factors that account for why something is known, we must also understand the practices that account for *not* knowing, that is, for our *lack* of knowledge about a phenomena or, in some cases, an account of the practices that resulted in a group *unlearning* what was once a realm of knowledge' (Tuana, 2006: 2) Further on she says: 'If we are to enrich our understanding of the production of knowledge in a particular field, then we must also examine the ways in which not knowing is sustained and sometimes even constructed. But just as our epistemologies have moved away from the dream of any simple calculus for knowledge, the elusive justified true belief, so too must any effort to understand ignorance recognize that it is a complex phenomena which, like knowledge, is situated' (2006: 2).
7 See also Steinberg's most recent book on genetics (Steinberg, 2015) – a brilliant, contemporary expose of the field.
8 See Ettorre, 2010a.
9 As is Ettore (2010b), written around the same time.
10 This is an old English expression. It means that no one talks to me – even in the corridors colleagues walk by me without recognising me or looking at me (see https://en.wikipedia.org/wiki/Send_to_Coventry)
11 See 'Introduction' in this this book.

References

Adams, T. E. (2011) *Narrating the Closet: An Autoethnography of Same Sex Attraction*. Walnut Creek, CA: Left Coast Press.
Adams, T. E. and Holman Jones, S. (2011) Telling stories: reflexivity, queer theory, and autoethnography. *Cultural Studies – Critical Methodologies* 11, 2: 108–16.
Barker, M. (2006) Critical sexology: sexual self-disclosure and outness in academia and the clinic. *Lesbian and Gay Psychology Review* 7, 3: 292–5.
Berry, K. (2006) Implicated audience member seeks understanding: re-examining the gift of autoethnography. *International Journal of Qualitative Methods* 5, 3: 1–7.
Bourdieu, P. (1984) *Distinction: A Social Critique of the Judgement of Taste*. Cambridge: MA: Harvard University Press.
Campbell, N. and Ettorre, E. (2011) *Gendering Addiction: The Politics of Drug Treatment in a Neurochemical World*. Houndsmills, UK: Palgrave Macmillan.
Crawley, S. (2002) They still don't understand why I hate wearing dresses! An autoethnographic rant on dresses, boats and butchness. *Cultural Studies ⇔ Critical Methodologies* 2: 69–92.
Crawley, S. (2008) The clothes make the trans: region and geography in the experiences of the Body. *Journal of Lesbian Studies* 12, 4: 365–79.
Eguchi, S. (2015) Queer intercultural relationality: an autoethnography of Asian–Black (Dis) connections in White gay America. *Journal of International and Intercultural Communication* 8, 1: 27–43.

Ettorre, E. (1980) *Lesbians, Women and Society*. London: Routledge and Boston, MA: Kegan Paul.
Ettorre, E. (1982) 'The perks of male power: heterosexuality and the oppression of women'. In Friedman, S. and Sarah, E. (eds.) *On the Problem of Men*. London: Women's Press, pp. 214–26.
Ettorre, E. (1992) *Women and Substance Use*. New Brunswick, NJ: Rutgers University Press and London: Macmillan.
Ettorre, E. (1997) *Women and Alcohol: From a Private Pleasure to a Public Problem?* London: Women's Press.
Ettorre, E. (ed.) (2001) *Before Birth: Understanding Prenatal Screening*. Aldershot, UK: Ashgate.
Ettorre, E. (2002) *Reproductive Genetics, Gender and the Body*. London: Routledge.
Ettorre, E. (ed.) (2005a) *Making Lesbians Visible in the Substance Use Field*. New York, NY: Haworth Press.
Ettorre, E. (ed.) (2005b) 'Introduction'. In *Making Lesbians visible in the Substance Use Field*. New York, NY: Haworth Press, pp: 1–5.
Ettorre, E. (2007) *Revisioning Women and Drug Use: Gender, Power and the Body*. Gordonsville, VA: Palgrave Macmillan.
Ettorre, E. (2010a) Nuns, dykes, drugs and gendered bodies: an autoethnography of a lesbian feminist's journey through 'good time' sociology. *Sexualities* 13, 3: 295–315.
Ettorre, E. (2010b) '*Autoethnography*: making sense of personal illness journeys'. In Bourgeault, I., De Vries, R. and Dingwall, R. (eds.), *Handbook on Qualitative Health Research*. Thousand Oaks, CA: Sage Publications, pp. 478–96.
Ettorre, E. and Riska, E. (1995) *Gendered Moods: Psychotropics and Society*. London: Routledge.
Foucault, M. (1984) *The Care of the Self. Vol 3: The History of Sexuality*. London: Penguin Books.
Gibson, M. and Meem, D. T. (2006) *Lesbian Academic Couples*. Binghampton, NY: Haworth Press.
Glassner, B. and Hertz, R. (eds.) (2003) *Our Studies, Ourselves: Sociologists Lives and Work*. Oxford: Oxford University Press.
Gust, S. W. (2007) Look out for the football players and frat boys: autoethnographic reflections of a gay teacher in a gay curricular experience. *Educational Studies* 41, 1: 43–60.
Inness, S. A. (1997) *The Lesbian Menace*. Amherst, MA: University of Massachusetts.
Joshi, S. (2007) Homo sutra: disrobing desire in the adult cinema, *Journal of Creative Work* 1, 2. Available at www.scientificjournals.org/journals2007/articles/1188.pdf (accessed 1 March 2016).
Krieger, S. (1996) *The Family Silver: Essays on relationships among women*. Berkeley, CA: University of California Press.
Macdonald, J. (2013) 'An autoethnography of queer transmasculine femme incoherence and the ethics of trans research'. In Denzin, N. K. (ed.), *40th Anniversary of Studies in Symbolic Interaction. Vol. 40: Studies in Symbolic Interaction*. Bingley, UK: Emerald Group, pp.129–52.
MacGregor, S., Ettorre, E., Coomber, R. and Crosier, A. (1990) *Drug Services in England and the Impact of the Central Funding Initiative*. London: Institute for the Study of Drug Dependence.
McNaron, T. (1996) *Poisoned Ivy: Lesbian and Gay Academics Confronting Homophobia*. Philadelphia, PA: Temple University Press.

Morris, T. (1957) *The Criminal Area: A Study in Social Ecology*. London: Routledge.

Munoz, J. (1995) The autoethnographic performance: reading Richard Fung's queer hybridity. *Screen* 36, 2: 83–99.

O'Byrne, P. (2007) The advantages and disadvantages of mixing methods: an analysis combining traditional and autoethnographic approaches. *Qualitative Health Research* 17: 1381–91.

Philareatou, A. and Allen K. (2006) Researching sensitive topics through autoethnographic means. *Journal of Men's Studies* 14, 1: 65–78.

Plummer, K. (2009) Autoethnography of sexualities: introduction. *Sexualities* 12, 3: 267–69.

Rose, H. and Hanmer, J. (1976) 'Women's liberation, reproduction and the technological fix'. In Barker, D. L. and Allen, S. (eds.), *Sexual Divisions and Society: Process and Change*. London: Tavistock, pp. 199–223.

Rutan, G. (1995) Catholic and Evangelical elites in dialogue and alliance. *International Journal of Social Economics* 22, 9–11: 109–34.

Smart, C. (2007) *Personal Life*. Cambridge, Polity Press.

Steinberg, D. L. (1997) 'Technologies of heterosexuality: eugenic reproductions under glass'. In Steinberg, D. L., Epstein, D. and Johnson, R. (eds.), *Border Patrols: policing the boundaries of Heterosexuality*, London: Cassell, pp. 66–97.

Steinberg, D. L. (2015) *Genes and the Bio-Imaginary: Science, Spectacle, Culture*. Farnham, UK: Ashgate.

Stoneall, L. (1981) Review of *Lesbians, Women and Society*. *Contemporary Sociology* 10, 4: 572–3.

Taylor, V. and Raeburn, N. (1995) Identity politics as high-risk activism: career consequences for Lesbian, Gay, and Bisexual sociologists. *Social Problems* 42, 2: 252–73.

Trotter, J., Brogatki, L., Duggan, L., Foster, E. and Levie, J. (2006) Revealing disagreement and discomfort through autoethnography and personal narrative. *Qualitative Social Work* 5: 369–87.

Tuana, N. (2004) Coming to understand: orgasm and the epistemology of ignorance. *Hypatia* 19, 1: 194–232.

Tuana, N. (2006) The speculum of ignorance: the women's health movement and epistemologies of ignorance. *Hypatia* 21, 3: 1–19.

Urla, J. and Terry, J. (1995) 'Introduction: mapping embodied deviance'. In Terry, J. and Urla, J. (eds.), *Deviant Bodies*. Indianapolis, IN: Indiana University Press, pp. 1–18.

Vannini, P. (2008) A queen's drowning: material culture, drama, and the performance of a technological accident. *Symbolic Interaction* 31, 2: 155–82.

2 Finding my feminist voice through an illness story
'An old female body confronts a thyroid problem'

> *Illness has always been of enormous benefit to me. It might even be said that I have learned little from anything that did not in some way make me sick.*
>
> (Walker, 1979: 370)

Beginning on a personal note

From February 2001 to September 2003 I suffered with an acute thyroid problem. This debilitating sickness robbed me of a vibrant feminist voice. When I got sick, I was on sabbatical leave, writing two books. My partner and I were recovering from the death of her father and dear sister. Soon after, my partner experienced a health crisis, which was at first thought to be fatal. Illness and death were all around me. I felt as if I had no space. I was afraid of life. My emotional pain was almost unbearable. But, I coped – not noticing subtle bodily changes, creeping up on me.[1] When I did, I thought 'menopause', reflecting how medical interpretations percolate into lay ones and how older women find it difficult to offer their own understanding of their condition or ask questions about its treatment (Lewis, 1993).

In this chapter, I frame my feminist autoethnography within the tradition of medical sociologists reflecting upon their own illness experiences (Adamson, 1997; Davis and Horobin, 1977; Frank, 1991, 1995; Rier, 2000; Roth, 1963; Zola, 1982). I want to employ autoethnography as a methodological tool for speaking and writing reflexively about my own illness experience of thyrotoxicosis. Naturally, I embed my reflections in feminist work, making connections between bodies, gender, illness, health and healing (Clarke and Olesen, 1999). As we are aware, chronic illness has a major impact on identity (Charmaz, 1983, 1990, 1991, 1999), is a radical intrusion into embodied selfhood (Turner, 1992) and is a well-researched area – but acute illness, such as thryrotoxicosis, is a neglected one.

My chapter reveals how this under-researched area gains from feminist analyses and from feminist autoethnography. I view my illness critically from the perspective of menopausal bodies constructed by biomedics. I also explore theoretically Foucault's (1984) concept, technologies of the self and Braidotti's (1994) feminist notions, nomadic flexibility and identifications. I do all this through my use of autoethnography as feminist methodology and I want to share my story with my readers.

Medical sociology and autoethnography

Because my story is an illness story, I initially look to medical sociology and its relationship to autoethnography through the work of Ellis and Bochner (1999). I find there are many authors, stories and readers. No conventional canons determine how illness stories should be constructed, but I must be thoughtful, reflexive, ethically self-aware, sensitive to gender, class, race and ethnicity in portraying others and evidence emotional reliability. My portrayals should depict the contours of the patient's sphere and the status of illness and health within that sphere. My stories should be flexible, in enough detail to express the realities of life and aesthetically alluring. I need to ensure explication of what is going on with others, even if their actions and perceptions of events, risks, infirmity, well-being, etc., differ dramatically from my own.

We saw in the Introductory chapter that autoethnography augments empathy on multiple levels including interactions between author and participants as well as reader and story (Bochner and Ellis, 2002). In a health and illness context, autoethnographies present particular embodied events with people in time, their social shaping and how these are representative of wider cultural meanings and social trends. Through its empathic form, autoethnography provides a tool to fashion a 'non-dualistic ontology' of the mindful body in which emotions play a central role in human experience and cultural scripts of health and sickness (Williams and Bendelow, 1996: 47).

Autoethnography allows both reader and author to enter into various textual strati and phases of illness understandings concerning what illness is and does, as well as what making meaning of illness involves. Do I dare contemplate risk, stigma and suffering alongside control, acceptance and victory? Do I interrogate myself as 'witness and doer' (Chawla, 2003)? Do I consider how the various people I encounter come to treat me in the way they do? What constrains them? What allows us to feel empowered as patients, physicians, nurses, etc.? 'Am I willing to include details that might reflect badly on me' (Berger, 2001: 514) and that might show me as an intransigent patient as well as stubborn? Similar to Frank (1995), Ellis's (2000: 273) optimal concern is, 'I want to think and feel with my story'. Although thinking and feeling with my illness story may be a novel challenge, autoethnography can help me to achieve this aim.

Ruminations of the 'healthy' once 'sick subject'

My autoethnography draws on data and analysis from diaries over two years when I suffered from thryotoxicosis. They include records of key events with times, places and people as well as feelings, emotions and bodily states (e.g. pulse rates, blood pressure and weight). I attach relevant articles, letters and blood tests to them. Before writing, I do an intensive study of my diaries. After my fourth reading and before data analyses, I write down all key events in a chronological order. This is difficult because remembering is painful and I feel desperate and lost. But I want 'to write from the heart, bring the first person in my work and merge art and science' (Ellis and Bochner, 2000).

Finding my feminist voice through illness 45

As I write, I stroke my neck and remember the thyroid pain and my fear of dying. I look out the window and stop stroking my neck. I have the feeling that as I remember key events, I am processing data through me as the now 'healthy' once 'sick body'. Although reading, remembering, writing and processing this data brings me emotional pain, I revisit my past by moving in and out of sad, painful experiences. I am moved to work harder. I begin to recall conversations and interactions that I had with 'significant others', such as my partner, friends, colleagues and doctors. I am excited because I am able to think and write clearly. But I feel vulnerable and alone. I am acutely aware that I interpret past events from my current position. I won't get it entirely right nor will I be able to represent these 'significant others' totally (Pyett, 2003). Ley and Spellman's (1968) classic work, demonstrating that the amount of information patients recall in communications with doctors is limited, looms in my memory. I am afraid, but I reassure myself, 'There is no such thing as getting it totally right. Seek verisimilitude. Evoke in your readers a feeling that your experience is described as lifelike, believable and possible' (Ellis, 1999: 674). I feel relieved. My story is about the past, constructed in the present. I confront specific biographical events, placing me in shifting relations of power with myself on the healing trajectory and others who provide different levels of care. I become aware that I am using the method of autoethnography to make sense of my illness experiences.

I do emotional recall[2] in which I imagine being back in these experiences emotionally and physically (Ellis, 1999: 675). Emotional recall is embedded in sociological introspection, a process accomplished in dialogue with the self and represented in the form of narratives (Ellis, 1991). It feels good – healing. Sociological introspection allows me to study my lived experiences not 'as an internal state but an emotional process which I recognise internally and construct externally' (1991: 32). This is bound up with my emotions and visceral reactions to others in specific sites and social exchanges. Although emotion work can be a way of reaffirming one's identity and managing the disruption of illness to one's biography (Exley and Letherby, 2001), I construct scenes and dialogue from partial descriptions in my diaries. I analyse them according to what each story says. I place them in a time line. I know my story is not totally accurate and certain events may be out of place but I press on. I know this work will take time but I feel satisfied. I am curious as to what I will find and how I will feel. I write and write and write. I have not only events before me but also situated settings, sites and conversations. I finish. I notice in my writing and analysing that a sense of triumph prevails. I have survived death. I have beaten this punishing illness. I feel overwhelmed with tenderness. I have suffered. I want to learn from my illness and explore the multiple subject positions experienced through my destabilised now stabilised and transformed healthy body. Yes, I am healthy now but a different 'healthy Betsy' than before I became ill. The cartography of acute illness has brought me 'health' but via a circuitous route, one that included choices to take an alternative path, leave my doctor and from the viewpoint of contemporary biomedicine, put myself at risk of more physical harm or even death.

Perhaps, in being focused on what my story is saying, I misrepresented what is going on for significant others. I found some of their behaviour difficult. My story is no less true than theirs. But it does provide comfort from my suffering in a way that differs from their biomedical way of expressing it (Ahlberg and Gibson, 2003). It gives me access to my experience of an unwelcome and painful process while allowing me to look more critically than these significant others at biomedical conventions and norms.

My illness journey from thryrotoxicosis to health

The beginning of symptoms: the body 'at war with itself'[3]

Mid-February 2001: I sit in my study asking myself, 'Why am I so floppy? I fall on the stairs. I've had terrible diarrhoea. Maybe it's food poisoning but I never had diarrhoea like this. It's probably because I am working too hard . . . Maybe it's menopause. I get palpitations and hot flashes . . .'. I am frightened of what is happening to my body. I am becoming not well and resisting this change. 'I don't want to die. Too many people around me just have'.

Thirteen days later I sit in a consultation room in front of Dr Walsh, my NHS[4] *GP (General Practitioner), a portly woman in her 40s with a kind face. 'Dr Walsh, I have been having bad diarrhoea for the past two weeks. I don't know what it is, which is why I came to see you', I say hesitantly. 'Could it have been something you ate?', she asks looking up from her notes. 'Well, perhaps. It did start after I had a spicy pasta', I say. She continues to write and says, 'Sometimes, food poisoning takes a while – weeks – to get out of your system. It's probably that'. I add in a worried voice, 'Also, I sometimes get these horrible hot flashes and palpitations too'. I notice that my right hand starts to shake violently. I quickly sit on it hoping that Dr Walsh doesn't see. 'Well, that could just be menopause. Would you like something for it?', she looks at me with pen in hand. 'No, I'd rather try control it through my diet', I respond.*

For the next three weeks I am on a work visit to Helsinki, Finland. My diarrhoea subsides for the first few days and comes back with a vengeance. I walk through the Helsinki streets, after presenting a University seminar, thinking, 'I wonder why I am so breathless all of the time. Must be the cold . . . I didn't feel nervous when I gave my paper, but I saw my hands shake. Strange really . . . I wish this diarrhoea hadn't come back. I need a loo wherever I go. I can't believe the hot flashes and palpitations. I hate this menopause feeling'.

Three weeks later I sit in front of Dr Walsh who appears to take a good look at me in between writing her notes. I try to make eye contact, 'I was away since the last time I saw you. For most of that that time, I had diarrhoea, but not for the past two days'. 'Have you been stressed lately?', she asks with concern. 'Not particularly'. I pause, 'Well yes, I am writing two books, why?' I ask quietly, returning the concern. 'Well, it could be psychosomatic – you could have the beginnings of irritable bowel syndrome', she says in an authoritative tone. 'Oh, I know that. My mother suffered from it for years', I say. 'Ah here it is', she says as she takes a small cylindrical container from her desk. 'I want you to take a stool sample to be sure you don't have an infection. 'Take this', she says as she hands me the container 'and bring it back tomorrow. We'll get it analysed. If it's clear, that's fine. Ring the surgery to find out. If it continues, we should get a blood test for you. Make an appointment with the nurse for that'. 'Thanks, doctor', I say as I stand at the door eager for this new plan of action.

Four days later I am ringing the surgery about the results of my stool test. 'The doctor says your stools are all clear', the receptionist responds. 'Thank you', I say as I hang up the phone. I think to myself, 'What a relief!' Two weeks pass . . .

The 'long in coming' diagnosis: 'Your thyroid's packed in'

'Dr Walsh said to see you for a blood test if my diarrhoea continues. My stools tested clear, but my diarrhoea has continued on and off. This week it's off', I say closing the door to the nurse's room. A short young woman in a blue nurse's uniform stands with her elbows resting on a sink full of plastic bags and says, 'Well, you don't need a blood test'. 'I wouldn't be so sure of that. This has been going on for some time', I say trying to disguise my surprise at her abruptness. I feel that I have to go to the loo. 'Let me go speak to the doctor', she says as she leaves the room. I wait quietly feeling nervous, but at least my bowels calm down. She returns. 'Dr Walsh says that you don't need the blood test.' 'OK, that is that', I say in a resigned voice.

Over the next six weeks, I loose weight even though I am eating like a pig. I should be relaxed because my writing is nearly finished, but I am not. I am nervous all of the time. My partner is beginning to notice. 'It feels as if a river is running through my body', I tell her one evening at dinner. I decide to go back to the nurse for a blood test. I know there is something wrong with me. 'I have come to get a blood test. My diarrhoea has not stopped', I say as I come into her room. 'So how long has this been going on for?' she asks. 'A few months now. I came here about five weeks ago. Then, Dr Walsh said that I didn't need a blood test. Don't you remember?', I ask feeling frustrated. The nurse opens the cabinet door above the sink. 'OK I'll get the syringe', she says.

Soon after, I receive a phone call from the receptionist telling me to see Dr Walsh. I sit in front of Dr Walsh whose manner seems rather upbeat when she comes smiling to fetch me from the waiting room. I say, 'You wanted to see me about . . .'. Before I am able to finish my sentence, she says, 'Yes, your thyroid has packed in'. 'What does that mean?' I say feeling immediately confused. She continues in a reassuring voice, 'Your thyroid is overactive. Your antibodies are attacking and destroying it. You are the second person today that has been diagnosed with this condition. The other is my father-in-law'. Sensing that she is in her element, I see her as the knowledgeable doctor. I think, 'She is trying to be friendly but at this moment I don't want to share my consultation with her father-in-law'. She continues, 'There are three options. We can cut the thyroid out. You can swallow radioactive iodine which kills it. Or you can take anti-thyroid tablets. I usually recommend the latter, carbimazole, which is perfectly harmless. What do you want?' I am confused and angry; I don't want to become chronically ill. I say, 'Well, I don't want surgery. The radioactive iodine doesn't sound too good. My mother has had cancer and I'd be afraid of taking anything if I am susceptible'. 'Oh there is no connection with cancer.

Radioactive iodine is perfectly safe', she retorts. A nervous laugh comes out of me and I say, 'I am not sure. I'll take the pills'. The prescription is handed to me as she moves her swivel chair towards me. 'I wonder when she wrote this', I think. She takes my wrist, 'Your pulse is 126, a little high[5] but this is to be expected. Just take the pills. Come in a month's time for a blood test and we'll review your dosage'.

Thirty minutes later I phone my partner. I tell her about my encounter with Dr Walsh, the diagnosis and prescription. I am worried and remember that my mother had the same condition. I decide to ring an alternative physician, Dr Fish, who my osteopath recommended once when I had hot flashes. My partner says reassuringly, 'That sounds like a good idea if you are afraid'. And I was.

Five minutes later I ring Dr Fish. I say that I received a diagnosis of overactive thyroid. I am afraid to take the pills my NHS doctor prescribed. I mention that I would like to explore the possibility of taking alternative medicine and to discuss this with her as soon as possible. Luckily, she has a time later in the day.

Six hours pass . . .

Uncertainty, risk and stopping orthodox treatment: taking the alternative path

I am at Dr Fish's private clinic. A stately looking woman enters, her right arm extended to shake my hand. She gives a penetrating look and guides me to her office. I feel her warmth immediately. 'Nice to meet you Professor Ettorre. Describe how you are feeling. I am sure we can sort something out, she says'. 'Not too well really. I feel as if a river is running through my body. I have terrible palpitations and diarrhoea. I am irritable. I can't sleep', I respond. She turns toward me and says, 'Tell me if you have had any poisoning recently'. 'No, I don't think so', I say with interest. In our conversation, she says that poisoning can cause thyrotoxicosis and if a patient's pulse goes too high, it can be life threatening, causing cardiac arrest. I find myself shuttering with fear but speak about the history of my diarrhoea, my other symptoms and my visit to Dr Walsh. She takes my pulse which is 120 and says that it is usual under these circumstances, but a normal pulse is around 60–70. She speaks about a patient who had the same condition and got better by taking an herbal remedy which she prescribed. She says that thyroid sufferers often feel as if they have no space to speak and asks if I feel that? I feel immediately very vulnerable and start crying softly. Tears run down my cheeks.

I respond, 'Yes, in a way'. I speak about recent grieving and sadness and say, 'You say a normal pulse is 60–70, well I am sure I have not had a normal pulse for some time'.

She looks quietly then says, 'I am going to prescribe you both homeopathic pills and a herbal remedy for the thryotoxicosis. You have to slow down and take time for yourself. Can you do that?' 'Yes, I am off on holiday in two day's time', I say. She asks to see me within three weeks. I tell her that is impossible because as soon as I come back from my holiday, I go to the US to attend some conferences. Looking horrified she says, "Well, that doesn't sound like a rest. You need to make sure you slow down. I would like your NHS GP's name. Also, you need to ring me while you are away to tell me how you are doing. I'll see you soon after you get back. You'll need to find out your blood test results. I am sure your NHS doctor will give them to you'. We agree that I'll ring her from my holiday.

While away, I take my pulse everyday and the range is from 81–124. I ring Dr Fish three times to say I am resting and feeling better. In Anaheim, California, I present papers at the Annual Conferences of the Society for the Study of Social Problems and American Sociological Association. I also attend the Annual Conference of Sociologists for Women in Society. Besides giving papers, I rest in the shade by the hotel swimming pool and dip in the cool water to relieve my symptoms. I see my colleagues walk past and greet me. I feel ashamed because I think they may see me as lazy.

On my return, I have a blood test taken by Dr Walsh's nurse. I ask her to give me the results of my first blood test. I say nothing about Dr Fish who I see soon after.

When I meet Dr Fish, I give her my blood test results.[6] The values are for free thyroxine,[7] 71.2 and thyroid stimulating hormone (TSH),[8] 0.01. Dr Fish says, 'You need to remember that herbal medication works slowly. If you take an anti-thyroid drug like carbimazole, it's like taking a sledgehammer to your thyroid. Herbal medication won't kill your thyroid. It works gradually but you need to slow down. Tell your NHS doctor that you have come to see me and that you are taking the herbal medicine. It is in your best interest to do that because if anything happens she is the one legally responsible. It is only fair that she knows'. I find myself becoming anxious but say quickly in response, 'OK, I'll do that'. Dr Fish notices my anxiety, 'You are a professional woman – a professor. I am sure you can talk with her'. I don't feel reassured but say, 'Yes, I am sure it will be fine'. We arrange another consultation in three week's time. When alone, I think, 'I'm an educated competent woman whose afraid of her GP – a first for me. When I read the next day that extreme nervousness and jangled emotions trouble 99 per cent of Grave's sufferers (Gomez 1994: 48), I understand.

A week later, I go to see Dr Walsh. I am anxious and hope she doesn't ask me about carbimozole. I can't bear to tell her about the herbal medication – jangled emotions again! I am shaking and feeling desperate. Looking at her notes, she says, 'We have the results of your blood test. Your free thyroxine is 55. It has gone down. Your TSH is the same. You don't need to see me any more. Take the medication and go to the nurse for blood tests and we'll monitor you that way.' I think, 'How different her consultations are from Dr Fish's'. I say, 'Thank you very much doctor. I am glad I am improving'.

The next week I meet with my Dean of Studies and say I am being treated for an overactive thyroid and want less work. He agrees, is very sympathetic and tells me his wife had the same condition. I am grateful for the understanding.

Five days later, I see Dr Fish. Tell her that my blood values are down. She says this is good news. Knowing that I start teaching, she says I need to pace myself because the herbal medication works slowly. She wants to know if I told Dr Walsh about taking it. Reluctantly, I say no because I was too frightened. Dr Fish volunteers to tell her but I say I'll do it. I am so scared about telling Dr Walsh about the herbal medication that I take carbimazole for a few days – these jangled emotions. I don't want to lie. I am sitting uncomfortably quiet with Dr Walsh's nurse in her treatment room a week later and say I've come for my blood test. Immediately she remembers. She gets the needle and starts taking blood from my arm. As she does, I say bracing myself, 'I am improving, um, I was taking herbal medication but now I am taking what Dr Walsh prescribed'. She finishes taking blood and looks up at me, 'Did I hear correctly? Why did you do that? Was it homeopathic medication? Let me hear your heart'. She puts the stethoscope on her neck to my chest and is visibly panicking. 'Your pulse is racing. I need to speak to Dr Walsh', she says rushing out of the room. I feel abandoned and a bad patient. Five minutes later, the nurse is standing in front of me, 'Dr Walsh is unhappy about your not telling her that you were taking herbal medication'. 'But, I have improved, I . . .', I begin to say. She cuts in with a scolding voice, 'It doesn't matter. You must go to the hospital and get an ECT. You have bad palpitations and these need to get seen to. You need to take beta blockers. You'll get a letter from the hospital. Promise you'll go this week'. Feeling demoralised, I say, 'Yes, I suppose', but I think to myself, 'Not on your life. I am never stepping foot in here again'. In my parked car, I ring Dr Fish. I ask to come to see her soon because I want her to help me to find a sympathetic NHS GP. We make an appointment in two days time. When we meet she tells me that what is happening is very stressful for me. She is concerned to get my pulse down and warns that I could have major health problems if it doesn't. I tell her about the nurse and how I took the carbimazole temporarily so as not to lie. She reassures me by saying that of course I can take it, if I choose to and she asks how it feels. I say I stopped and that for the first few days, it was OK. But soon after I got terrible headaches, my pulse and my blood pressure shot up and the palpitations were violent. She suggests that she take my next blood test and she'll sort me out for a sympathetic GP. On her desk is a book of registered physicians who are trained in homeopathy. She looks through it and gives me a list of names.

That same evening, I ring the names on the list. One doctor is unable to help because I am outside of his catchment area, but he gives me the phone number of Dr Edwards, a trained homeopath as well as an NHS GP in my area. The next day I ring Dr Edwards's surgery, find out the address and go personally to register. I make an appointment to see him after he returns from his holiday.

Sometimes, I feel like I want to die.

A month passes . . .

Increasing pulse rates and heightening work pace: the 'inflexible body'

My blood test from Dr Fish shows my values going down. I see Dr Edwards and tell him about my overactive thyroid, my herbal medication from Dr Fish who he knows of and about leaving Dr Walsh because she wants me to take carbimazole. Dr Edwards is a man in his mid-40s whose weathered and open face I am immediately drawn to. Looking at me directly, he says in a soft voice, 'To be honest, carbimazole is not pleasant and can have dangerous side effects. Unfortunately, it's the most common drug we use for overactive thyroid. If a patient does not want to take a drug, she shouldn't. It's your body, not mine. You shouldn't feel forced to take a drug. But one thing we were told is that homeopathic medicine doesn't work for thyroid conditions'. I breathe a sigh of relief. I feel comfortable with this man. 'I am using homeopathic remedy but mainly a herbal medication and I am taking 15 drops three times a day', I say. He begins to write and looks up asking, 'How are your blood values? Are they improving?' 'Yes. I feel better than when I was first diagnosed. He continues, 'I am a little unclear. Did you ever take carbimazole?' 'Yes, for a few days but I felt sick with it. I felt as if my eyes were popping out', I say. Our conversation continues in a calm manner. Dr Edwards suggests that I continue to take my herbal medication, have my blood tests with his phlebotomist and copy my results to Dr Fish. He agrees to monitor my progress and asks me to consider sick leave and he will sign me off.[9] He asks to see me in a few weeks and thanks me for coming. I leave feeling elated because he is empathetic. 'Just what I need', I think.

A month later I go to the phlebotomist who is a young nurse with a professional manner. She explains what she will do and shares that she has an underactive thyroid. After she takes my blood, she asks me to ring the receptionist for my results. When I leave, I notice how calm I feel as well as satisfied.

A week later, I receive my results which show an improvement. My free thyroxine is 24.9, but the TSH is the same. I see Dr Fish and tell her the news and about meeting Dr Edwards. She notices my tremor and my right eye is slightly bulging, a classic sign of overactive thyroid. She asks me if I want an eye specialist and I say I am trying to avoid traditional doctors. She laughs and says, 'You must be relieved now that you met Dr Edwards. I was concerned because just going to a doctor can cause stress and this is what we want to avoid'.

Two months pass . . .

The decision to take the healing journey: skis, yoga and sick leave

My free thyroxine levels go up while the TSH remains the same. I go on a trip to Lapland for Christmas with friends and feel well enough to ski. On my return, I have a blood test and see Dr Edwards. He tells me that I am not yet normal. I mention that I'd like to take sick leave for three weeks and he agrees saying, 'That is fine. I'll sign you off'. While I am on sick leave, I go to see my osteopath who suggests that I try yoga because I have a frozen shoulder which is common in thyrotoxicosis. I phone the yoga teacher and tell her that I have an overactive thyroid and I think yoga would help. Immediately she tells me that her sister had the same problem and yoga helped. She asks me to come this evening and I agree. Immediately after class, I notice my pulse goes down.

I want to do everything I can do to get better. Dr Fish suggests that I have my amalgam fillings in my teeth removed. I have them replaced, a process which takes six months. I eat organic food, do yoga regularly, drink very little alcohol, take my pulse daily and 'pace' myself. I renew an old activity – 'doing nothing'. This involves me sitting and literally doing nothing. That is how I used to calm myself when I was younger. Perhaps, as I become older and busier, I become ill because I forgot how to calm myself. I find 'doing nothing' healing. I am able to sit back and think about my life. It is a 'reflective' luxury for me. I become an advocate of 'looking after oneself' and talk with colleagues about how all of us in the academy need to slow down in our stress-filled lives.

Almost a year passes . . .

Avoiding the thyroid storm through normal hormones: 're-embodying' health

I am feeling much better. The palpitations stop. My pulse is down. In January, I go for a blood test. By this time, I agree that I ring the phlebotomist directly for my results. In mid-February, I am abroad at a meeting and during a short break; I ring the phlebotomist. After I hear her voice I say, 'Hi it's me Elizabeth. Do you have my results?'

She responds quickly saying, 'Yes, let me find them'. There is a long pause and shuffling of paper. 'OK Elizabeth, here they are – 15.2 your free thyroxine and 0.46 your TSH. They are normal'. 'That is great', I say with joy. 'Do you know this is the first time my TSH is normal since I started having my blood tests almost 18 months ago?' 'No, Elizabeth I didn't. That is very nice to hear,' she responds excitedly. 'Congratulations', she adds. I feel full of delight. 'OK, I'll see you at my next blood test and thanks', I say before I hang up.

Eight days later I am with Dr Fish who wears a lovely floral dress with a matching scarf. The sun is shining through the window onto her desk. I am smiling. 'Good news, Dr Fish I am finally "normal"', I say. She smiles too. 'Well done. I knew you would do it. So all of your discipline has paid off. I must tell you', she says as she looks over my notes. There is a long but pleasant pause. 'I am just looking at your notes from our first consultation'. She looks up, "When you first came to see me, you had all the symptoms of acute thyrotoxicosis. I was very worried about you. You could have easily gone into what we call "thyroid storm",[10] had a cardiac arrest or even died. I just kept my fingers crossed that you would pace yourself so you would go slower. I am very pleased for you . . .'. I smile and feel deep joy . . .

'Doing thyrotoxicosis'

Hopefully, you, the reader will have seen from this that autoethnography is a useful method of making sense of an acute illness experience. In the following discussions, I want to turn the readers' attention to theoretical concerns. For example, I want to discuss how accounts of acute illness, which are shaped by biomedical constructions of gendered bodies and rely on notions of a unitary illness identity, mastered if not tyrannised by health, are challenged by deconstructing 'gendered thyroids'. I introduce the notions, technologies of the self, nomadic flexibility and identifications.

Gendered thyroids, emotions and menopause

In Britain, hyperthyroidism (another name for thyrotoxicosis) affects 2 per cent of women and 0.2 per cent of men (Gittoes and Franklyn, 1998). In the US, the ratio of female to male is 4 to 8.1 (Ansar *et al.,* 1985, cited in Martin 1999: 102). Although more women than men are affected by thyroid disorders, experts perpetuate misconceptions about women's thyroid glands as being more vulnerable to the vagaries of their emotions than men's. A physician writing on thyroid disorders says that a woman's emotional system is more susceptible to upset than a man's and that there are two periods when a woman is particularly vulnerable to this kind of upset: after giving birth and during menopause (Gomez, 1994: 10). This reveals the subtle gendering of susceptibility to thyroid disorders within the medical profession. The belief is that anybody's (i.e. a man's or woman's) thyroid interacts with stress hormones, but a woman's have a greater propensity to disorders. This 'essentialist' viewpoint is based on the assumption that a woman's metabolism is more complex and delicate than a man's and women are more responsive to the effects of their emotions than men (Gomez, 1994 :10).

This essentialist viewpoint is consistent with the mind–body dualism of Western biomedicine. Regarded by physicians as ruled by her emotions, the female body becomes a metaphor for the body pole of this dualism, 'representing nature, irrationality and sensuality', in contrast to the male body, the mind or normalised position of 'social power, rationality and self-control' (Davis, 1997: 5). In the binary narrative of biomedicine, physicians perpetuate gender stereotypes about emotions and label hormones as if they were intrinsically gendered (Birke, 2000: 592). The health effects of these misconceptions are clear: women's health takes second place in toxicological studies (Birke, 2000: 594) or when their illnesses are purported to be linked with emotions, for example when a woman suffers from hyperthyroidism during menopause.

In my autoethnography, these misconceptions came to life when my thyroid symptoms were dismissed by my physician as 'psychosomatic' and/or 'menopausal'. Although these dismissals did not benefit my state of health, I take a wider perspective and consider the social implications of them.

Technologies of the self, nomadic flexibility and identifications

In the beginning of my story, I experience classic thyrotoxicosis symptoms. Gradually, the symptoms become worse. My routine narrative about the status of my own health is being disrupted as I move increasingly into reconstruction mode (Williams, 1984). I attribute my symptoms to the stress of writing two books on sabbatical, but I also clock up difficult life experiences. I am in grief. Although there are alternations in my thyroid, I am myself 'alterative'; these minute bodily movements hint at embodied adjustments in my appearance, physical tenacity and psyche. My right eye bulges out. I feel weak. I eat like a horse. I loose weight. I can't think.

By way of these alterations, the small butterfly shaped gland in my neck draws my body silently into organic degeneration. The process of losing myself (Charmaz, 1983), the workings of my discursive consciousness and, most importantly, hegemonic views and images of myself as an ill, menopausal woman are set into motion. I must lack discipline or did not give my immune system enough training to be rewarded in the currency of health (Martin, 1994: 327). My female body is obstinate. If I don't slow down, I won't get better. It is as simple as that. I have to learn how to 'pace' myself.

By the time my thyroid has 'packed in', I am in the process of losing the body I know. At the same time, I entertain an imaginary relationship to my once healthy body. 'She' is still here, as are my partner, my friends, my work colleagues, my doctors, etc. To change embodiment is to change identity (Turner, 1992: 256). I am unsure. The difficulty I have with this and other 'identity notions' in the 'masculinist'-dominated field of medical sociology is that there is little, if any, room for technologies of the self (Foucault, 1984) where gendered individuals create their own identities through ethics and forms of self-constitution (Best and Kellner, 1991: 61).

For example, because I am turning out to be unhealthy, if my identity is an identity of a sick person, an identity which becomes threatened (Coyle, 1999), has a disrupted biography (Bury, 1982) and a reconstituted narrative (Williams, 1984), needs identity work (Strauss *et al.*, 1982) and has a restricted life (Charmaz, 1983), my identity appears as somewhat fixed. More importantly, my identity is judged against exclusionary standards of normativity (including gender) in everyday life. Within these 'problematizations of illness identities', chronicity is prioritised over acuteness as well as health over illness. As an overarching regime, medicine as a voluntary and rational structure of conduct (Foucault, 1984: 100) takes control of my gendered illness existence. What specific disciplinary practices, besides being categorised as infirm, are available to me for transformation to a healthy, desiring female body? How do I approach the moral problem of my body that I have to address (Frank, 1995)? What technologies of self are at work in my desire if not passion towards health?

In my autoethnography, I effect sometimes by my own means and sometimes with the help of others a certain number of technologies or embodied practices. I visit doctors. I have my blood taken. I take advice. I don't take advice. I rest. I take herbal medication. I learn yoga. I have jangled emotions. I express anger. I express joy. I do nothing. All of these I do in order to attain a state of health which I seemingly have lost. If Charmaz (1983) is able to transform a restricted medicalised view of the chronically ill person's pain into a broader view of suffering, sociologists in a quest for a greater understanding of health and illness should create wider, more stylised 'infirmity identities' and gendered embodiments that defy closure, while resisting scopic regimes (such as medicine) which authorise and legitimate a morality of health.

Aware of my triumph (i.e. I had survived) as well as tenderness (i.e. I had suffered), I wanted to learn from my illness experience and explore the multiple selves experienced through my destabilised, infirmity identity[11] that I embodied. Disenchantment with the dominant Cartesian paradigm of rationality at the heart of modern medicine (as well as the social sciences) leads me to narrative because, as I noted in the Introduction, 'narrative emphasizes plurality of truths' that subcultures and cultures claim about themselves (Bell, 2000: 132). I want to move far away from notions that a single cultural perspective, revealing unquestionable truths to be known or told exists *and* that any scholar is able to achieve an understanding of illness experiences outside of specific historical contexts or without recognition of shifting relations of power and inequalities. In this way, my autoethnography generates useful ways of creating knowledge about infirmity identities – identities suffering and grappling with the intricate, interior language of wounding, despair and moral pain, as well as the victory of living an illness.[12]

Thus, if I abide by narrow conceptions of myself as 'ill', how am I able to embrace new forms of embodiment, pleasure, pain and desire in my illness experience? In asking this question, I challenge sociologists to take up the feminist position of 'nomadic flexibility', embedding us in a critical consciousness that resists settling into socially coded modes of thought and behaviour and relinquishes all idea, desire or nostalgia for fixity (Braidotti, 1994: 22). This position emphasizes identifications more than identity.

Braidotti (1994: 166) contends that 'Identity is a play of multiplicity, fractured aspects of the self; it is relational, in that it requires a bond to the other; it is retrospective, in that it is fixed through memories and recollections, in a genealogical process'. Identity is related to the unconscious and differs from wilful choice. How conceptions of myself and my 'identifications' are produced is key here (Scott, 1991). If my conceptions are made up of successful identifications of myself as ill or healthy, I am primarily the one who makes these identifications in relationship to significant others. But, most importantly, these identifications are unconscious internalised images that escape rational control. If my body, ill or healthy, can't really be fully apprehended, how can my 'identity'? One way I survive is to use technologies of self in my attempt to constantly adjust notions of my own embodiment to the internalised images of the whole female body that I am. In this context, my autoethnography hints at my own internal contradictions, confusions and uncertainties when I pay attention to the level of identity as complexity and multiplicity (Braidotti, 1994: 166). I feel like I want to die; I feel like I want to live. I am able to do nothing, to do something, be well while feeling ill, be ill while feeling well, be the object of my 'identity' and the subject of my unconscious. On the one hand, I resist pathologisation. On the other hand, I embrace wholeheartedly regularised blood tests for corporeal assessments, assigning me specific pathological values, providing others with standards for biomedical normalisation.

As a practice, holding on to identifications not identity was strategic for me as evidenced in my story. That finally somebody, first Dr Fish and then Dr Edwards, sees the entirety of my symptoms – not merely the diagnostic entity – (see Frank, 2002) is crucial in my journey. I am a multiple, fractured body, even though I am a whole 'sick body'. My bodily changes lead to a thematisation of my corporeality, a visceral sense of embodiment in which bodily strangeness becomes a part of my life (Kvinge and Kirkevold, 2003). In this process, embodied adjustments are made for me. Doctors tell me what to ingest. My yoga teacher tells me how to breathe. A nurse extracts blood from my veins. I make embodied adjustments for myself. I nourish my illness as 'acute' by rejecting carbamizole; I 'stave off' chronic illness. When I do nothing, I feel something different than before when I did nothing. I increase herbal medication to decrease the size of my thyroid. My wounded gendered body becomes a reflexive body 'capable of ruminating, deliberating, cogitating, studying and thinking carefully' (Martin, 2003: 356). The dominant 'identity' of 'healthy body', no longer as important as earlier, recedes in my consciousness, and yet my embodied identifications become those of liminality, in betweeness and are flawlessly cultural.

In conclusion, this chapter began with the premise that autoethnography is a helpful method of telling illness stories as well as creating sociological insights into patienthood, in particular older female patienthood. Conceptualising uncertainty and at times conflict between an older female patient and her health professionals within autoethnography can bring new insights to understanding and explaining this type of uncertainty and these conflicts. What happens when acute illness strikes a menopausal body unfolds, and, similar to Alice Walker's epigraph that opens this chapter, this illness was of 'enormous benefit to me'. In learning about the multiple contours of embodied illness and health, I want to help others who want to think and feel with their stories. For me, attempting 'to write from the heart' has been one small step in sensitising my feminist 'I' by finding my lost feminist voice and, with a bit of luck, helping others to do the same.

Notes

1. These symptoms included palpitations, joint pains, general muscle weakness, falling, sleeplessness, weight loss, shaking (tremor), 'gritty' eyes, discolouration of the skin on my neck (vitiligo), diarrhoea, irritability, high pulse, damp skin, brittle nails, dull hair, hair loss, swollen neck and difficulty in swallowing.
2. Please see the Introduction for an explanation of the importance of emotional recall and also endnote 12 in the Introduction.
3. Texts in italics are data based on extractions from my diaries over the past two years.
4. NHS is the National Health Service, the British state-funded health service.
5. This is my resting pulse. I am twice the normal rate.
6. Blood values vary between laboratories. At mine, the normal range for free thyroxine is between 2.8–23.1 and for TSH, 0.35–5.5. (I am three times the normal value).
7. This is the tiny but significant part of the main thyroid hormone. Its level in the blood is useful in assessing whether the thyroid is functioning properly (Gomez, 1994: 119).
8. TSH is produced in the pituitary gland and directs the thyroid to produce hormones. TSH goes up when the thyroid isn't providing enough . . . and down when there is a surplus (Gomez, 1994: 119).
9. In order to get statutory sick pay in Britain, it is a requirement that your NHS GP 'signs you off work'.
10. This is overactivity of the thyroid that has run out of control. With it, one becomes critically ill.
11. See Clarke and Olesen (1999: 10) for a discussion on how there are 'multiple selves' and 'multiple subject positionings in the heterogeneous cartographies of contemporary life'. Although Clarke and Olsen refer mainly to the dynamics of race, gender and class, I extend their analyses to include the cartography of 'sick/healthy bodies'.
12. Besides living with an illness, I am also aware that being a woman academic has affected my autoethnography. Through my autoethnographic reflections, similar to Hernández et al. (2010: 11), I learn 'how social, cultural, and institutional changes scaffolded' my academic identity and understand more 'what the role is of the historical context, the power relationships, and the gender issues in the construction of my personal and professional identities'.

References

Adamson, C. (1997) Existential and clinical uncertainty in the medical encounter: an idographic account of an illness trajectory defined by inflammatory bowel disease and avascular necrosis. *Sociology of Health and Illness* 19, 2: 133–59.

Ahlberg, K. and Gibson, F. (2003) Editorial: 'What is the story telling us?'. Using patient experiences to improve practice. *European Journal of Oncology* 7, 3: 149–50.

Bell, S. E. (2000) 'Experiences of illness and narrative understandings'. In Brown, P. (ed.), *Perspectives in Medical Sociology*. Prospect Heights, IL: Waveland Press, pp. 130–45.

Berger, L. (2001) Inside out: narrative autoethnography as a path toward rapport. *Qualitative Inquiry* 7, 4: 504–18.

Best, S. and Kellner, D. (1991) *Postmodern Theory: Critical Interrogations*. New York, NY: Guilford Press.

Birke, L. (2000) Sitting on the fence: biology, feminism and gender-bending environments. *Women's Studies International Forum* 23, 5: 587–99.

Bochner, A. P. and Ellis, C. (eds.) (2002) *Ethnographically speaking: autoethnography, literature and aesthetics*. Walnut Creek, CA: Altamira Press.

Braidotti, R. (1994) *Nomadic Subjects: Embodiment and Sexual Difference in Contemporary Feminist Theory*. New York, NY: Columbia University Press.

Bury, M. (1982) Chronic illness as biographical disruption. *Sociology of Health and Illness* 4, 2: 167–82.

Charmaz, K. (1983) Loss of self: a fundamental form of suffering in the chronically Ill. *Sociology of Health and Illness* 5, 2: 168–95.

Charmaz, K. (1990) Discovering chronic illness: using grounded theory. *Social Science and Medicine* 30, 11: 1161–72.

Charmaz, K. (1991) *Good days, bad days: the self in chronic illness and time*. New Brunswick, NJ: Rutgers University Press.

Charmaz, K. (1999) 'Discoveries of self in illness'. In Charmaz, K. and Paterniti, D. (eds.), *Health, Illness and Healing: Society, Social Context and Self: An Anthology*. Los Angeles, CA: Roxbury Publishing, pp. 72–81.

Chawla, D. (2003) Two journeys. *Qualitative Inquiry* 9, 5: 785–804.

Clarke, A. E. and Olesen, V. L. (1999) 'Revising, diffracting and acting'. In Clarke, A. E. and Olesen, V. L. (eds.), *Revisioning Women, Health and Healing*. New York, NY: Routledge, pp. 3–48.

Coyle, J. (1999) Exploring the meaning of 'dissatisfaction' with health care: the importance of 'personal identity threat'. *Sociology of Health and Illness* 21, 1: 95–124.

Davis, A. and Horobin, G. (eds.) (1977) *Medical Encounters: The Experience of Illness and its Treatment*. London: Croom Helm.

Davis, K. (1997) 'Embody-ing theory: beyond modernist and postmodernist readings of the body'. In Davis, K. (ed.), *Embodied Practices: Feminist Perspectives on the Body*. London: Sage Publications, pp. 1–23.

Ellis, C. (1991) Sociological introspection and emotional experience. *Symbolic Interaction* 14, 1: 23–50.

Ellis, C. (1999) Heartful ethnography. *Qualitative Health Research* 9, 5: 669–683.

Ellis, C. (2000) Creating criteria: an ethnographic short story. *Qualitative Inquiry* 6, 2: 273–7.

Ellis, C. and Bochner, A. (1999) Bringing emotion and personal narrative into medical social science. *Health* 3: 229–37.

Ellis, C. and Bochner, A. (2000) 'Autoethnography, personal narrative, reflexivity: researcher as subject'. In Denzin, N. K. and Lincoln, Y. S. (eds.), *Handbook of Qualitative Research*. Thousand Oaks, CA: Sage Publications, pp. 733–68.

Exley, C. and Letherby, G. (2001) Managing a disrupted lifecourse: issues of identity and emotion work. *Health* 5, 1: 112–32.

Foucault, M. (1984) *The Care of the Self. Vol. 3: The History of Sexuality*. London: Penguin Books.

Frank, A. (1991) *At the Will of the Body: Reflections on Illness*. Boston, MA: Houghton Mifflin.

Frank, A. (1995) *The Wounded Storyteller: Body, Illness and Ethics*. Chicago, IL: University of Chicago Press.

Frank, R. (2002) Integrating homeopathy and biomedicine: medical practice and knowledge production among German homeopathic physicians. *Sociology of Health and Illness* 24, 6: 796–819.

Gittoes, N. J. L. and Franklyn, J. A. (1998) Hyperthyroidism: current treatment guidelines. *Drugs* 55, 4: 543–53.

Gomez, J. (1994) *Coping with Thyroid Problems*. London: Sheldon Press.

Hernández, F., Sancho, J. M., Creus, A. and Montané, A. (2010) Becoming university scholars: inside professional autoethnographies. *Journal of Research Practice* 6, 1: Article M7, 11–15. Available at http://jrp.icaap.org/index.php/jrp/article/view/204/188 (accessed 3 April 2016).

Kvinge, K. and Kirkevold, M. (2003) Living with bodily strangeness: women's experiences of their changing and unpredictable body following a stroke. *Qualitative Health Research* 13, 9: 1291–310.

Lewis, J. (1993) Feminism, the menopause and hormone replacement therapy. *Feminist Review* 43: 38–56.

Ley, P. and Spellman, M. S. (1968) *Communicating with the Patient*. London: Staples Press.

Martin, E. (1994) *Flexible Bodies: The Role of Community in American Culture from the Days of Polio to the Age of AIDS*. Boston, MA: Beacon Press.

Martin, E. (1999) 'The woman in the flexible body'. In Clarke, A. V. L. (eds.), *Revisioning Women, Health and Healing*. New York, NY: Routledge, pp. 97–115.

Martin, P. Y. (2003) Said and done versus saying and doing: gendering practices, practicing gender at work. *Gender and Society* 17, 3: 342–66.

Pyett, P. M. (2003) Validation of qualitative research in the 'real world'. *Qualitative Health Research* 13, 8: 1170–9.

Rier, D. (2000) The missing voice of the critically ill: a medical sociologist's first-person account. *Sociology of Health and Illness* 22, 1: 68–93.

Roth, J. A. (1963) *Timetables: Structuring the Passage of Time in Hospital Treatment and Other Careers*. Indianapolis, IN: Bobbs Merrill.

Scott, J. (1991) The evidence of experience. *Critical Inquiry* 17: 773–97.

Strauss, A., Fagerhaugh, S., Suczek, B. and Weiner, C. (1982) Sentimental work in the technologized hospital. *Sociology of Health and Illness* 4, 3: 54–78.

Turner, B. (1992) *Regulating Bodies: Essays in Medical Sociology*. London: Routledge.

Walker, A. (1979) *I Love Myself When I Am Laughing – A Zora Neal Huston Reader*. New York, NY: The Feminist Press.

Williams, G. (1984) The genesis of chronic illness. *Sociology of Health and Illness* 6, 2: 175–200.

Williams, S. and Bendelow, G. (1996) 'Emotions, health and illness: the missing link in medical sociology'. In James, V. and Gabe, J. (eds.), *Health and the Sociology of Emotions*. Oxford: Blackwell Publishers, pp. 25–53.

Zola, I. (1982) *Missing Pieces: A Chronicle of living with a Disability*. Philadelphia, PA: Temple University Press.

3 Doing feminist autoethnography with drug-using women

> *Those of us who stand outside the circle of this society's definition of acceptable women; those of us who have been forged in the crucibles of difference – those of us who are poor, who are lesbians, who are Black, who are older – know that survival is not an academic skill. It is learning how to take our differences and make them strengths. For the master's tools will never dismantle the master's house. They may allow us temporarily to beat him at his own game, but they will never enable us to bring about genuine change. And this fact is only threatening to those women who still define the master's house as their only source of support.*
>
> (Lorde, 1984: 111)

As a feminist researcher, I am excited because I want to use autoethnography as a way of bringing my drugs research alive for my readers. I have been in the drugs field for many years and have not used autoethnography before now. Having said that, I was delighted in 2011 to read Dina Perrone's (2010) article, 'Gender and sexuality in the field: a female ethnographer's experience researching drug use in dance clubs'. In it, she introduces autoethnography as a way of giving more attention to the embodied researcher in the field, albeit I would have liked to see more evidence of 'emotional recall'[1] in her piece. Regardless of Perrone's article, I am aware that autoethnography is still controversial within the field of qualitative research (Dingwall, 1992) and that using 'an emotional narrative mode of autoethnographic writing' goes against established canons in social science research, specifically in the area of health research[2] (Ellis and Bochner, 1999) and, I would add, the related field of drug research. Often, I find in the peer review process, some reviewers doubt the 'truth' of my research or accuse me of being 'self indulgent' or 'narcissistic'. This chapter brings me as a feminist autoethnographer squarely into the drugs field and it begins with a sense of encouragement, joy and expectation. I see myself as having an excellent opportunity to demonstrate why autoethnography is a useful way of doing not only drugs research but also feminist research with female drug users that involves dialogical exchanges as 'data'.

This chapter includes a series of inter-related discussions. I begin with a discussion of how in my earlier work I noted the emergence of two related but disparate genres of speaking about oneself in the field of health research. Second, I turn the reader's attention to the 'methods and data' in this particular autoethnography.

I want to demonstrate a way of seeing autoethnography as a useful methodological tool for speaking and writing reflexively about one's experiences as a feminist drugs researcher. Third, I tell my stories about doing drugs research with drug-using women and the intricate emotions and embodied reactions involved. Fourth, I want to explore the ways that autoethnography contributes to an overall analysis of particular kinds of problems associated with the issue of reflexivity and how feminism engages with these problems. Included within this discussion is a related discussion on the issues of reliability and validity and how autoethnographers view these issues. Last, I want to make some conclusions by asking the question, 'where do we go from here?'

In earlier work (Ettorre, 2005, 2006), I argued that specifically within health sociology two related but disparate genres of speaking about oneself appear: 'modernist observers' and 'postmodernist witnesses'. I noted that these genres are not a strict binary: a few 'modernist' accounts hint at 'postmodern' autobiographies to come.[3] Nevertheless, although both genres can be seen as autobiographical narratives, it is the postmodernists who are receptive to the vagaries of narrators' experiences and 'labileness' of their embodied emotions. The 'postmodern witnesses' are more open to research that moves away from universalistic conceptions of respondents and embraces multiple, embodied forms of narrative representations, replete with uncertainties. This postmodern turn goes beyond monolithic notions that a single cultural perspective, revealing a certain arrangement of truths to be known, exists. Postmodern witnesses bring the body, emotions, participation and existential uncertainty into the research arena. In a real sense, postmodernist witnesses deploy a type of 'anti-narrative' (Scholes, 1980) which frustrates closure, bringing performative codes (Denzin, 2003, 2006) to our critical attention and seeing these codes as cultural rather than fixed aspects of human life.[4] As feeling, embodied and vulnerable observers, postmodernist witnesses give voice to the structured silence of embodied experiences, as well as social and cultural shape to the diverse, complementary and conflicting assistance that the experience of the self and the body brings to one's personal narratives.

In this chapter, my autoethnography draws on data and analysis from transcriptions of narratives and research notes from visits to four women drug users.[5] As shown in my earlier autoethnographies, my notes include records of key events with times, places and people as well as feelings and emotions. The stories of drug-using women used in this chapter come from the 'mountain of words' (Johnson et al., 2010) produced in this study. Before writing, I do an intensive study of transcriptions of narratives and research notes. After my third reading and before data analyses, I write down all key events in a chronological order. This is difficult and trying because difficult emotions come to the surface for me. It feels like this will be a challenge because I am so used just to writing up research results and not using my emotions in my drugs work. As I said, I have been in the drugs and alcohol field for many years. All the difficult experiences that I have had as a feminist researcher are now reappearing. I am not sure why now, but these difficult emotions are here and I have to face them and feel them. My transcripts do make remembering easier. However, remembering is somewhat disturbing for me because my experiences were at times difficult and emotionally draining. I am certainly 'writing from my heart' (Ellis and Bochner, 2000).

As I write, I remember the melancholy I shared with these four drug-using women. I look out the window and stroke the computer keys. I am starting to have a deep sense of sadness. I have the feeling that as I remember key events I shared with these women, I am processing data through my body as the now 'sitting on my own in front of my computer' feminist drugs researcher. It is hard because the melancholy pervades my being. Although reading, remembering, writing and processing this data brings me sorrow, I revisit the past by moving in and out of these sad, painful experiences. I am inspired by these women to drudge on. I am also energized because I know their voices will be heard if I listen to them. Except, I feel weak. It's so hard because the autoethnographer does not get any story wholly accurate. Facts and conversations may change, but I am aware and that is OK. I can be fearful but I must also encourage myself through authenticity (Ellis, 1999: 674).[6] I feel thankful. My story is about remembering the doing of this drugs research in the past, but I am building my analysis in the present. I am using the method of autoethnography to make sense of these acutely felt, research experiences with drug-using women. It feels good to use emotional recall (see Endnote 1). All of what I am going through now, what I am feeling is all about the emotions I felt and the instinctual responses I made with these women whilst doing my research. I structure these emotions and responses as I remember them emerging from the social spaces and conversations I had with all of these women. Some conversations appear as unfinished explanations or descriptions in my research notes. I examine them according to what each woman was saying to me – her wholehearted responses. I am able put these exchanges in various points in time. All this work takes a lot of time and energy. It demands patience, steadfastness and curiosity. I notice in my writing and analysing a sense of success predominates, and yet in being focused on what my stories are saying, I found sadness within each story. But then again, my story is no less real than the women I speak with. As I noted earlier,[7] I need to be ethically accountable to methodological principles of how I portray the people around me in my autoethnography. The sources of data are research notes and transcribed conversations with women with whom I speak and who give me informed consent.[8] I feel as if I am beginning to find my voice and these women's voices. I am aware that only when I find my voice can these women find theirs in my narratives. These voices emerge and possibly merge as I begin to write my social science prose. We create dialogical exchanges in relationship and display how our research conversations are always a give-and-take – a pull of emotions and a sharing of realities altered in these research exchanges. Now, I will go on to their stories.

The stories of Mary, Cheryl, Hilary and Jean[9]

Mary's story (9 September 2005)

As I arrive outside Mary's home I think, 'This is a rather run down area'. Mary's[10] *red brick house is rather depressing looking. Eager to speak with her, I feel excited* and I knock on her door. A squat, solid woman with short mousy brown hair opens it. She looks me up and down and says with a distinctive working class accent, 'You're Betsy, Nicky[11] said you'd visit. Come on in'. 'Thanks', I say feeling shy. Mary directs me to a red couch. Smiling, she sits on a large green armchair directly across from me. I realise that the situation feels somewhat contrived. I am not feeling very relaxed. Perhaps, sensing my discomfort, Mary stands up and asks, 'Do you want a cup of tea?' I answer, 'Yes' happy for the brief time to gather my thoughts. 'Let Mary speak', I say to myself as she hands me a mug of steaming tea. In our exchanges, Mary speaks about how using heroin 'makes her mellow'. She says, 'It's just so easy . . . heroin . . . you love it . . . I've been around it all my life . . . I've got two brothers who's (sic) heroin addicts . . . It made me feel safe when I was taking it'. I am enchanted as I was aware that heroin may 'make one mellow' but over the years few drug users have admitted this to me. So this revelation is interesting for me and I am feeling intrigued. Later, I learn another side to Mary's drug use as she talks about 'her worst drug experience': 'You . . . skip to the lowest . . . when you're trying to get that fix . . . do anything . . . Well for me . . . I . . . got into crime to feed my habit . . . I was driving people around . . . They were shoplifting. I was watching . . . so they didn't get caught. I was lucky . . . I ain't (sic) one of the girls . . . having to sell themselves on the streets. I wouldn't do anything like that because I've got Cathy[12] . . . Most end up working on the streets . . . prostitution . . . Quite a few . . . started [out] with me a couple of years ago . . . I'm lucky. I've got . . . quite a nice home . . . my daughter. I've got everything . . . They've got nothing . . . [Their homes] . . . you wipe your feet when you walk out. It's that bad . . . I ain't (sic) gone down that road. Even though I was low because I was doing heroin . . . Cathy still comes first.

As I listen to Mary, I feel conflicting emotions – very sad because this woman has had many obstacles to overcome to be a 'good drug using mother'. On the other hand, I am joyful to see that she is a real survivor. I am particularly moved when she talks about being a 'single mum' and how 'when you are a lone parent and a drug addict, no one gives you the time of day . . .' 'It's easier for a man to go out', she says as she twirls her hair around her finger, . . . I'm a single parent so I've got to be at home . . . The man can go out because the best time 'to feed'[13] is during the night . . . I can't . . . go out in the . . . night . . . They'll . . . go out . . . taxing[14] somebody . . . selling heroin . . . it don't matter to them . . . if they need the money . . . they . . . get it within five, ten minutes . . . Me, I've got to think about it in the morning . . . to score . . . Men don't care . . . They've got more balls . . .

As I listen I am curious about her views on male users and find out unfortunately that she has experienced domestic violence. This makes me feel very sad. She says, 'If you're with some scum of a bloke and he wants his fix then he'll batter you until you get outside and earn yourself some money by working on the streets . . . I'm lucky that I'm not in a relationship. . . . I was . . . a few years ago . . . I was battered . . . cos I wouldn't go working on the streets and that was for amphetamines . . . wasn't for heroin . . . He [her former partner] said, 'A woman can open her legs whereas a bloke can't get out there . . . sell themselves' . . . No woman's after a bloke, it's always the other way around. Feeling empathy for Mary, I shut off the recorder as she asks, 'Do you want another cup of tea?'

Cheryl's story (28 September 2005)

At the drugs centre, Nicky brings me into a counselling room. Sitting there on a new IKEA chair is a pretty woman with dark brown eyes and short black hair. She looks in her mid-20s and is smiling at us. Nicky says, 'Cheryl, this is Betsy. You said it was OK to speak with her'. Nicky exits the room. I ask Cheryl, 'Were you waiting long?' 'No', Cheryl said looking with big eyes, 'I just arrived myself'. In our conversations, I learn that Cheryl is 24, says she has been 'clean for 2 years' and has had two admissions at rehabilitation centres, one in the local area and one in London. Her drug of choice is heroin; a drug she was first 'turned on' to five years ago when visiting Los Angeles. She was arrested a few times. Her experience Stateside ended up as a 'disaster' and while she worked in the States, she hasn't worked since she left hospital there. Currently, she is waiting to hear about a youth worker course.

    Settling myself comfortably in my chair, I ask tentatively, 'Where shall we begin, Cheryl? Nicky says you have a lot to tell'. Cheryl says spontaneously, 'I moved around a lot . . . It was a bit chaotic. . .'. 'Tell me about it', I say feeling curious. 'Well', she says looking directly at me, 'I started to use heroin with [friends] . . . with Linda, my girlfriend . . . I . . . did [heroin] instead of coke . . . for a couple of weeks. [When] I tried to stop using . . . : I was starting to . . . withdraw . . . I thought, ". . . Too late, it's got me". I didn't care . . . I was just enjoying . . . the heroin . . . [I] could feel . . . the warmth going . . . through [my body] . . . This was bliss'. Again feeling inquisitive, I ask, 'When did your problems start?' Looking at me in a strained way which signalled to me that her experience was painful, she says, 'I got an abscess . . . It didn't come up like a normal abscess . . . my shoulder swelled up. . . I thought it would go away. . . [that] I had flu . . . I was getting . . . feverish . . . convulsing . . . I was having more and more heroin . . . to stop it . . . I couldn't eat . . . everything I was drinking I was puking straight back up . . . nothing would stay in my stomach . . . That went on for . . . three weeks . . . I was getting heroin from this Mexican guy . . . I didn't go to work . . . Then . . . two people came over . . . took me to this café. I had a bowl of soup . . . started to shake . . . We went into the toilet . . . I had a bit of heroin. That didn't affect me at all . . . I . . . knew something was . . . terribly wrong . . . I just collapsed'. I am feeling cheerless and think how terrible this experience was for her. I learn that Cheryl ends up being admitted to hospital and has septicaemia. She is told that she damaged her liver. Although Cheryl was 'happy to stay in the hospital' because she was 'getting pain killers', her sister who lives in LA visits her and alerts her parents. She is flown back to the UK and goes to a London clinic. She says, 'I think that London was a lot worse than America. In America I had money, I'd been working, the heroin was good. In London I waited ages . . . for benefits . . . I was having to do . . . shoplift[ing] . . . mixing with dodgy people. I felt a lot more vulnerable to being ripped off by drugs dealers because I wasn't a man. I didn't have that back up of muscle . . . Shoplifting was the same. I used to go with a guy . . . He could intimidate the store detective into not coming . . . after me . . . I got arrested a few times . . . I got let off on a conditional discharge. In my rehabilitation house, they did . . . reverse psychology with me . . . They . . . gave me my freedom to be responsible for myself . . . They let me out . . . on my *own... It totally worked... Six months and I completed... I did have some good friends in there... we moved into a... house together... I'm dying to get back into work now... I'm frustrated not doing anything here... Sometimes it's hard to think that that was me, but... that was just another stage in my journey... I've... got to know myself for the first time in my life...'. Feeling tired, I smile and say, 'Thanks, Cheryl'.*

Hilary's story (10 October 2005)

Nicky takes me to an old, depressing Victorian building that houses social services. Through the front door, she escorts me to a tiny room. I am feeling a mixture of excitement and fear. A young woman with dark skin and a beautiful face sits on a shabby blue couch. With a gloomy face, she looks up as we enter. Nicky says, 'Hilary, this is Betsy who I told you about'. Nicky moves to the door and exits saying, 'I'll be next door'. The room is rather miserable and painted a sickly green. Immediately, I feel depressed. I sense I'm not the only one and say quietly, 'Can you tell me about yourself. Nicky told you I am interested in talking with women drug users'. 'Sure', Hilary responds, 'I am 35, have a 3-year-old son who was taken from me when I was arrested for possession'. Not wanting to disturb the quiet atmosphere, I nod asking, 'What happened?' She continues, 'There was a raid... the police... pretended they were Parcel Force... I was upstairs... my son was being got ready for nursery... [a] Jamaican guy... was there... to take him to nursery... At 8.30 am... there was this knock... they said, "It's a parcel"... Fifteen officers came running in... laid me on the bed... I... was so scared... straight away I said, "The drugs are under the pillow"... I've been involved with drugs for... many years... it isn't me... to do the things I've done'. She touches her tearful right eye and continues, 'My son was taken off me... He's been in care ever since. Until a month ago, people thought I'd go to prison'. I listen with empathy and learn that Hilary doesn't go to prison. Her life is a series of traumas. Remembering she speaks slowly, 'It started off with alcohol, then cannabis, Tipp-Ex, solvents... I was raped when I was... on cannabis at fourteen... I went to speed... I'm very weight conscious... I started off with a food disorder from the age of... five... I've always had mood swings, but during the years of drug addiction... when you go into rehab you'll find that the doctors... say, "Well, it must be drug related"... The mood swings... depression and... eating disorder was (sic) there well before the drugs... I was brought up in a... middle-class family. I had nannies... I never felt that I fitted in... [After] boarding school it was punk... I was accepted... speed came into my life but emotionally I had already gone off the rails... I had a serious leg operation[15]... so my parents decided that I stay in London'.

Sorrowfully, I learn that gaining support as a drug-using mother has been variable for Hilary. She continues, 'Last year, I left [rehabilitation house]... with a 2-year-old son who I'd never been with on my own... He was conceived through a rape... crack addict... because I'd been in... an environment with support... I was saying [to] social services, "I'm going to need this".... They didn't give a damn. I didn't get... support... but they started doing some work with me... I get supervised now . . . they haven't got any problems with my parenting . . .'. I sigh with relief. Hilary talks about how she wants more 'women-only rehabs' because 'every rehab I've been in I get into relationships'. She 'wants to go in to a detox just where there's women'. . . 'A man will ask me for sex . . . I can't say no'. She was raped in rehab and 'lost her confidence'. For her 'women-only places would be totally different'. I ask her what the future will bring and she says with sadness in her voice, 'I want my son . . . I'll do anything. But I know deep in my heart at the moment I can't do it . . . I . . . honestly . . . feel . . . I . . . need . . . help . . . to give me a month away from everything . . . little bit of clean time . . . It's all about my son . . . to give him . . . quality I need some time out'. We both look at each other and I smile with a sad heart. 'I hope everything works out for you Hilary', I say with sadness in my voice. I leave the room slowly and search for Nicky.

Jean's story (12 October 2005)

Nicky and I go to a local drug clinic situated on hospital grounds. As we walk into a dark foyer, the atmosphere is chaotic,[16] A woman with ginger hair, a worn face and bedraggled clothes comes out from behind a locked door as a buzzer sounds,[17] 'Hi' she says and looks timidly, 'You must be Betsy'. 'Yes', I say smiling attempting to look composed but disturbed by the atmosphere. Sitting down in one of two chairs in the foyer, she continues, 'Let's have a chat now'. Surprised that we are stuck in the foyer, I look at Nicky who walks away saying, 'I'm going for a coffee. Sit down Betsy'. Jean gazes at me with expectation, 'You wanna know about me (sic) drug use'. 'Tell me when you started', I say curiously. Jean is 32 and got into drugs when her son was five[18] and was 'chased out' of her home because she 'was one of the first people to get into gear' in her home town. She worked the streets.[19] Suddenly, a loud scream comes from reception. Startled, both of us look up. 'Fuck that's Sue', Jean says. 'How about we go over there?' I say pointing to a small alcove 20 metres away with perspex windows and soft red chairs. After we settle, I begin to feel comfortable but sad – sensing that Jean's life is tough. She continues, 'My partner[20] is inside . . . I'd be on the street . . . with his burglaring . . . we'd have two lots of money . . .'. 'When did his troubles begin?', I ask carefully so as not to disturb the somewhat peaceful atmosphere in the alcove.

'[One day] George [a dealer] came round . . . offered John work. I didn't want John to take it . . . We got a car . . . It saved me from going . . . on the street . . . George . . . worked John into the ground . . . from 9 am till 10 pm without a break . . . One day John made him six grand'. 'So', I ask quietly, 'what happened next?' Jean continues, 'Some woman phoned George . . . said we mucked about with the crack. We hadn't . . . but George took her word . . . He nearly cut John's face. John . . . caught his hand otherwise he would have had a big mars bar[21] . . . Next morning John said, "We're going. I've got two and a half grand worth of stuff". . . . I thought he was joking . . . I was . . . to stay behind . . . Lucky I didn't 'cos my sister's boy got stabbed in the leg three times . . .'. Anxiously, I ask, 'If he catches you what would he do?' 'Oh, he'll stab me', she says calmly, 'He's . . . told [his] girls'.[22] Suddenly I feel overwhelmed, rub my eyes with force. 'Are you OK?', *she asks. 'Sure', I reply. She continues, 'John never wanted me to do it [sex work]. I didn't want him to go out [burgling] . . . He knew he was likely to get nicked . . . because . . . we always had the police around . . . He always . . . gets big bird[23] so that's why I did it[24] . . . He doesn't like me doing it . . . I've been attacked . . . got stabbed . . . 3 years ago . . . He never got caught'. My heart goes out to Jean. I say softly trying not to appear patronising, 'How do you find it here?' She looks at me with sad eyes, 'It's a big change . . . When I got here . . . I nearly . . . walked out. I've been in prison twice'. I ask, 'Does John know you are in here?' 'Yes, he's proud of me', she responds. 'He got three and a half years . . . be out in January . . . That's why I've got . . . to get my life sorted out. [I] can't carry on like this. . . . I don't want to be 40 and still on drugs . . . I've had enough . . . It's doing my head in. I've got to do it for myself, my son . . . for John. . . . If we don't get our lives sorted out, the next one's his third strike and he could get life for it . . . The other day . . . he said, "Tell Nicky not to worry about me, cos I'm sorting myself out"'. . . . She is nearly crying now. I take her cold hand saying, 'I'm sure it will all work out for you'. A loud bang comes from reception. Our heads turn quickly around. 'It must be the iron door at reception', I think.*

A feminist researcher does autoethnography in the field of drugs

In the following discussion, I want to turn our attention to some key theoretical concerns. As shown throughout all the chapters in this book, autoethnography is a 'reflexive methodology', which emphasizes the need for critical reflection on behalf of researchers with respect to the production of narratives. Especially for feminist researchers, we need to be vigilant about being reflexive and to use our work as a way of committing to the future of women. As reflexive researchers, we must acknowledge how our social, cultural and disciplinary positioning has shaped our narratives (Heapy, 2007: 44). Alvesson and Sköldberg (2000: 7–8) contend that there are four elements in reflective research in which social science researchers (and I would add feminist drugs researchers) should be engaged, regardless of the specific methods he or she prefers. These include (1) techniques in research procedures with well-reasoned logic in interacting with one's data; (2) an understanding of the primacy of interpretation; (3) awareness of the political–ideological character of one's research and (4) recognition of the problem of representation of 'the text' and authority of the 'researcher'.

Feminist autoethnography contributes to an understanding of the kinds of problems one faces when doing reflective research and, more specifically, reflection per se. Reflection is the interpretation of interpretation and the launching of critical self-exploration of one's own interpretation of empirical material, including its construction (Alvesson and Sköldberg, 2000: 6). Autoethnographers are involved deeply with reflection, while the process of doing autoethnography engages them with Alvesson and Sköldberg's four reflective areas in a direct, if not visible way. However, as feminists we can add to these notions and borrow from Haraway (1994: 62) who argues that we need to go beyond 'reflection and its variants in doctrines of representation'. She argues that creating our critical theories is not totally about reflexivity, 'except as a means to defuse the bombs of the established disorder and its self-invisible subjects and categories (1994: 62)'. Haraway uses the 'optical metaphor' of 'diffraction – the non-innocent, complexly erotic practice of making a difference in the world, rather than displacing the same elsewhere'. For example, in constructing my research stories, I, as an autoethnographer, may follow the narratives of myself with others in a process of reflexive narrative making, but I also need to deflect what I see and force these ideas into society. Although I may demonstrate a well-reasoned logic in using the 'conversations' with women drug users as my research texts, my stories become my 'data'. On the other hand, I do not have a fixation on data or claim that my stories mirror reality exactly. They are diffracted by a barrage of emotions and embodied subjectivities. I must divert thinking that these women are hopeless or not worthy of life in society. My focus may be on how best I am able to study 'the researching culture' that involves me and the women with whom I am conversing. But I must also show the limitations of this researching culture, which I believe autoethnography does. Regardless of the fact that I have been a 'reflexive' autoethnographer, there is always an explicit recognition of the significance of interpretation in producing autoethnographies, as well as the need to challenge the orthodoxy concerning drug use in society. I may commit myself to insuring a level of authenticity in my research text and help the reader to gain a sense of emotional reliability in the story (Ellis and Bochner, 2000: 749). However, emotional reliability also depends on whether or not I am able to set off 'the bombs of the established disorder'. The political–ideological character of autoethnographic research is explicit in that as an autoethnographer, I must appraise not only my own emotions, bewilderment, uneasiness[25] and uncertainty but also demonstrate why different cultural interests (i.e. doing drugs research with women) are preferred or not. I recognise that my cultural assumptions and interpretations are not neutral but themselves construct political and ideological conditions within which the story itself will be interpreted by others (see Alvesson and Sköldberg, 2000: 8).

Recognition of the problem of representation of 'the text' and authority of the 'researcher' is not an overwhelming problem for authoethnographers. This is because the research text lives its own life, separate from me, the author. It carries its own force of diffraction. It is in the creation of the text that it is always disengaged from me, the author; and yet the text entangles me and others as readers and story participants into the experiential web of the drugs orthodoxy as well as an anti-orthodoxy. Nevertheless, as a vulnerable self and an autoethnographic author I am able to move in and out of the text as writer, observed, observer and participant and never as 'truth sayer'. I am merely 'a storied subject' among others. I don't want to represent the drugs orthodoxy and as a feminist, I am challenging established truths about women drug users as I go along. Although there may be a sense of wholeness to my story, there will always be evidence of fragmentation and chaos. For autoethnographers, there is a profound risk involved in projecting one's private emotions onto a larger cultural scene. In this sense, the quandary of precarity replaces the problem of representation. For myself, I found 'parallel narratives' shaping the conversations I had with women drug users. Although women drug users have consistently been viewed as 'abject' and less than non-drug using women, my 'story' 'parallels' theirs in that I have consistently felt vulnerable, worthless and and less than a 'real' researcher because I have studied women drug users and championed their cause. Following Haraway, I have tried to make a difference in the world.

When we start to question the truth of our data or the truth claims of researchers, we approach the delicate issue of validity and whether or not our accounts represent the social phenomenon that we study. For Ellis (2004: 124), she looks at 'validity in terms of what happens to readers as well as to research participants and researchers' (i.e. our autoethnographies seek verisimilitude). Autoethnography strives for generalizability not just from the respondents but also from the readers (Ellis, 2004: 195) and intends to open up rather than lock down discussion (2004: 22). Concerning the issues of both reliability and validity, autoethnographers also view the former issue as being linked with self-consciousness and the integrity of one's stories and the latter with the emotional integrity of the author; how reflexivity operates, acknowledging how one's knowledge, position and experience shape one's analysis (Cho and Trent, 2006: 331; Pyett, 2003: 1171) as well as the emotional reliability of the story, its aesthetic appeal and most important, its usefulness in augmenting empathy (see Sandelowski, 2004: 1373). I'd like to go a step further and argue that if we want to make a difference in the world we, as autoethnographers, need to challenge how reflexivity operates. Not only can we never truly 'know' what goes on around us in the complexity of our research worlds but also we can only be reflexive if we dare to be relation to others. In turn, this 'daring relatedness' shapes deflects, spreads, bends and diverts convoluted understandings and misunderstandings of ours and others' embodied subjectivities. We only make critical theory if we dare to go beyond established doctrines of representation and authenticate or validate ourselves.

Sparkes (2001) argues that if validity is played down as is happening as new forms and approaches to enquiry emerge within qualitative research (including autoethnography), the struggle for legitimacy may revolve around what constitutes valid research. Sparkes (2001: 549) argues for a type of coexistence between different types of 'validity perspectives' and entices researchers to have a respectful acknowledgement of the differences between alternative forms of inquiry in terms of their process and products so that each could be judged using criteria that are consistent with its own internal meaning structures. Certainly, if this sort of coexistence were initiated it would mean that autoethnography would be accepted not only as a reformulation of ethnography but also a reformulation of what it means to theorise the social and cultural (Clough, 1997) in today's world. Here, it is important to remember that there is no canonical approach to autoethnography and thus, it is not possible to determine when it is appropriate or not appropriate to use autoethnography.

Where do we go from here?

In conclusion, this chapter has been based on the premise that autoethnography is a helpful feminist method of telling research stories as well as creating social and cultural insights into the lives of women drug users. I began with a discussion on how autoethnography is part-and-parcel of the postmodern turn in the social sciences. I explored how to do autoethnography in the field of drugs use; asked questions about the evidential value of autoethnographic material; looked closely at how autoethnography contributes to an overall analysis of particular kinds of problems related to reflexivity and diffraction and showed how I was able to theorise the social and cultural in my 'doing drugs research' story.

One key theme of the chapter was to show the reader that similar to other autoethnographers (Tedlock, 2000: 468), autoethnographers in the drugs field are able to clarify and authenticate their self-images and feelings through writing reflexive stories. The reader saw glimpses in my own autoethographic work that I desired to become a communicative body (Frank, 1995) and experienced 'parallel narratives' with those I researched. Whether or not I have achieved this level of generosity, I have through autoethnography 'given voice to my body' (Sparkes, 2003a: 64),[26] experienced a connectedness to others (Richardson, 2001), especially women drug users, and bore witness to how embodied identifications with others are able to induce dialogical exchanges.

In these dialogical exchanges, I used autoethnography with women drug users because I wanted to demonstrate how the research process is always a giving and receiving, an ebbing and flowing of information, a closing off and opening up of emotions and different realities. I specifically wanted to focus on women drug users because like the women that Audre Lorde speaks of in the epigraph for this chapter, these women also 'stand outside the circle of this society's definition of acceptable women . . . and . . . learn how to take . . . differences and make them strengths'. Thus, I was moved emotionally by the stories I heard: Mary's 'mellowness' as a lone parent; Cheryl's past disaster as helping her to create present insights; Hilary's thoughtfulness as a mother and victim of violence and Jean, the sex worker turned 'patient' in a 'locked' drug clinic. I saw these women's lives as deeply human and, most importantly, as a demonstration of the embodied pain and tragedies that are emblematic of women drug users – selling bodies, sick bodies, stabbed bodies, anorexic bodies, weeping bodies, violated bodies, pregnant bodies, injecting bodies, 'cracked up' bodies, scared bodies, scarred bodies, sick bodies, broken bodies, oppressed bodies, female bodies, raped bodies, bodies perceived as 'bad bodies' by society (see Ettorre, 2007; Campbell and Ettorre, 2011). We need to show that drug use has a major impact on identity and is as a radical intrusion into embodied selfhood (Ettorre, 2007) for both the researched and the researcher. Thus, in learning from these women's narratives about the multiple contours of embodied drug use *vis-à-vis* their womenhood, let us continue to use autoethnography in the drugs field. I want to challenge outdated methodological canons that deny us as autoethographers our voice. Let us set off the methodological and theoretical 'bombs' of 'the established disorder'.

Notes

1 As noted in the Introduction chapter, emotional recall helps the researcher to imagine being back in key events emotionally and physically and is embedded in sociological introspection (Ellis, 1991, 1999). Perrone (2010) reveals more about what happened

Autoethnography with drug-using women 71

around her as a researcher and less about how she felt when those events were happening. The reader does not have a full sense of how Perrone was feeling, which is slightly disappointing.
2 As we saw in Chapter 2.
3 In my previous work, I argued that by giving testimony to what has been traditionally abject in illness accounts, 'postmodern witnesses' make way for new and perhaps more reflexive, gender sensitive ways of doing patienthood. In a specific medical sociology context, researchers tell illness narratives because telling gives us therapeutic benefits of redemptive understanding but also the 'political consequences of connecting the body to the self, reveals embodiment and emotionality as legitimate mediums of lived experience, inscribing bodily dysfunction with value' (Bochner, 2001: 148; see also Ettorre, 2009).
4 We saw in the Introduction how autoethnography fulfils a performative role. When I am telling my story, I am committed to transmitting my dream of feminism – facilitating my readers to amalgamate feminist ways of thinking and practice into their daily lives. Thus, feminist autoethnographers are a fundamental part of postmodern witnessing.
5 In mid-2005, I mounted a small pilot study called 'Women users' core activities in the illegal drug culture' inspired by Tammy Anderson's (2005) work. Initially I was interested in looking at how women appear in the drug world in different ways to men and the connections between women's pursuits in the illegal and conventional worlds. I was able to recruit to the study five current and former women illegal drug users through a local drugs agency worker. However, I was only able to talk with four women because the final respondent cancelled due to her being admitted to a rehabilitation house. My 'conversations' with these women lasted about 2–3 hours each and were carried out either in the respondent's homes or private rooms in rehabilitation homes, social services or drug agencies/clinics. These 'conversations' took place over four weeks between 9 September to 12 October 2005. Because these 'conversations' brought very painful emotions to the surface for both myself and the drug-using women respondents, I focused the study on my personal experience of doing these exchanges. Placing this work in an autoethnographic context, I wanted to consider how to theorise 'the research text' and with the backdrop of empathy and sorrow, detail the research choices I made and the participatory framework in which these were set. I was unable to do this research without ethical approval and this study was given ethical approval on 3 September 2004 by the South and West Devon Research Ethics Committee (REC).
6 See also Chapter 2.
7 See the Introduction.
8 This was a requirement when I received ethical approval for doing this research. (See Endnote 5 above.)
9 All names used in this chapter have been changed.
10 Mary is a 33-year-old mother with a 9-year-old girl. Until recently, she has been using heroin on a daily basis for 2 years and has also used amphetamine and cannabis. She doesn't have a partner and comes from a family of drug users, all living in the local area.
11 Nicky was the local drugs worker and key contact for me in this study. She helped me to recruit these women drug users for my study.
12 Her 7-year-old daughter.
13 To rob or steal.
14 'Taxing somebody' is when money or drugs are taken from people who are dealing for 'protection' and control purposes. It can also be a mugging set up by a dealer who gets his mugger to rob the 'runner' or lower level dealer he has just sold to. This means that the lower level dealer then owes the main dealer money for the drugs whilst retaining the drugs that his mugger returns to him.
15 Hilary was run over when she was ten and her leg was broken. As a result, one leg grew and one didn't and her spine and hips were 'becoming uneven'. The operation was 'to even them up' otherwise she was told she would have 'problems in life'.

16 There were two nurses and about five patients talking loudly in a large room located near reception. 'Perhaps, it was a patient group', I thought. Additionally, a patient with a raised voice was arguing with a nurse in the reception area.
17 I presume this means that drug users as patients are locked in the clinic.
18 Jean has a 16-year-old son from a previous marriage. She let him go with his dad because 'They were going to take him off me because they found out he had a burn on him. My husband told them [social services] that I'd burnt him, which was not true.'
19 As a sex worker.
20 John.
21 A cut down his face.
22 George is also a pimp.
23 Prison time.
24 Sex work.
25 Perhaps, I am also anxious following from Crawford's (1996: 163) observations, which I partly share: 'For me . . . We go into the field. We place ourselves in some social setting. We may even ask the "natives" to take us in or, better yet, be invited without asking. I am skeptical about this. Even though I am deeply intrigued with human behavior and thoroughly enjoy reading ethnographic accounts . . .'.
26 Sparkes (2003a, 2003b) shows the devastating sense of loss when injury shapes a performing athletic body into 'a failed' disabled one.

References

Alvesson, M. and Sköldberg, K. (2000) *Reflexive Methodology: New Vistas for Qualitative Research*. London: Sage Publications.
Anderson, T. L. (2005) Dimensions of women's power in the illicit drug economy. *Theoretical Criminology* 9, 4: 371–400.
Bochner, A. (2001) Narratives' virtues. *Qualitative Inquiry* 7, 2: 131–57.
Campbell, N. and Ettorre, E. (2011) *Gendering Addiction: The Politics of Drug Treatment in a Neurochemical World*. Houndsmills, UK: Palgrave Macmillan.
Cho, J. and Trent, A. (2006) Validity in qualitative research revisited. *Qualitative Research* 6: 319–40.
Clough, P. T. (1997) Autotelecommunication and autoethnography: a reading of Carolyn Ellis's 'Final Negotiations'. *Sociological Quarterly* 38, 1: 95–110.
Crawford, L. (1996) Personal ethnography. *Communication Monographs* 63, 2: 158–70.
Denzin, N. K. (2003) *Performance Ethnography: Critical Pedagogy and the Politics of Culture*. London: Sage Publications.
Denzin, N. K. (2006) Pedagogy, performance and autoethnography. *Text and Performance Quarterly* 26, 4: 333–58.
Dingwall, R. (1992) '"Don't mind him – he's from Barcelona": qualitative methods in health research'. In Daly, J., McDonald, I. and Willis, E. (eds.), *Researching Health Care: Designs, Dilemmas, Disciplines*. London: Routledge, pp. 161–75.
Ellis, C. (1991) Sociological introspection and emotional experience. *Symbolic Interaction* 14, 1: 23–50.
Ellis, C. (1999) Heartful ethnography. *Qualitative Health Research* 9, 5: 669–83.
Ellis, C. (2004) *The Ethnographic I: A Methodological Novel About Autoethnography*. Walnut Creek, CA: Altamira Press.
Ellis, C. and Bochner, A. (1999) Bringing emotion and personal narrative into medical social science. *Health* 3, 229–37.

Ellis, C. and Bochner, A. (2000) 'Autoethnography, personal narrative, reflexivity: researcher as subject'. In Denzin, N. K. and Lincoln, Y. S. (eds.), *Handbook of Qualitative Research*. Thousand Oaks, CA: Sage Publications, pp. 733–68.

Ettorre, E. (2005) Gender, older female bodies and autoethnography: finding my feminist voice by telling my illness story. *Women's Studies International Forum* 28: 535–46.

Ettorre, E. (2006) Autoethnography: making sense of my illness journey from thyrotoxicosis to health. *Auto/Biography* 14: 1–23.

Ettorre, E. (2007) *Revisioning Women and Drug Use: Gender Power and the Body*. Houndsmill, UK: Palgrave Macmillan.

Ettorre, E. (2009) 'An autoethnograpy of "being healthy without feeling healthy": re-thinking the "older" lesbian "identity"'. In. Powell, J. and Gilbert, T. (eds.), *Ageing and Identity a Postmodern Dialogue*. New York, NY: Nova Science, pp. 57–68.

Frank, A. (1995) *The Wounded Storyteller: Body, Illness and Ethics*. Chicago, IL: University of Chicago Press.

Haraway, D. J. (1994) A game of cat's cradle: science studies, feminist theory, cultural studies. *Configurations* 2, 1: 59–71.

Heapy, B. (2007) *Late Modernity and Social Change: Reconstructing Social and Personal Life*. London: Routledge.

Johnson, B. D., Dunlap, E. and Benoit, E. (2010) Organising 'mountains of words' for data analysis, both qualitative and quantitative. *Substance Use and Misuse* 45: 648–70.

Lorde, A. (1984) The master's tools will never dismantle the master's house. *Sister Outsider: Essays and Speeches*. Berkeley, CA: Crossing Press, pp. 110–14.

Perrone, D. (2010) Gender and sexuality in the field: a female ethnographer's experience researching drug use in dance clubs. *Substance Use and Misuse* 45: 717–35.

Pyett, P. M. (2003) Validation of qualitative research in the 'real world'. *Qualitative Health Research* 13, 8: 1170–9.

Richardson, L. (2001) Getting personal: writing stories. *Qualitative Studies in Education* 14, 1: 33–38.

Sandelowski, M. (2004) Using qualitative research. *Qualitative Health Research* 14: 1366–86.

Scholes, R. (1980) Afterthoughts on narrative: language, narrative and anti-narrative. *Critical Inquiry* 17, 1: 204–12.

Sparkes, A. (2001) Myth 94: qualitative health researchers will agree about validity. *Qualitative Health Research* 11: 538–52.

Sparkes, A. (2003a) 'Bodied, identities, selves: autoethnographic fragments and reflections'. In Denison, J. and Markula, P. (eds.), *Moving writing: crafting writing in sport research*. New York, NY: Peter Lang, pp. 51–76.

Sparkes, A. (2003b) 'From performance to impairment: a patchwork of embodied memories'. In Evans, J., Davies, B. and Wright, J., (eds.), *Body Knowledge and Control*. London: Routledge, pp. 157–72.

Tedlock, B. (2000) 'Ethnography and ethnographic representation'. In Denzin, N. K. and Lincoln, Y. S. (eds.), *Handbook of Qualitative Research*. Thousand Oaks, CA: Sage Publications, pp. 455–86.

4 'She wrote it but look what she wrote'

> What an honor and privilege to work with Tony and Stacy . . . the best dream team imaginable. They work hard and efficiently, challengingly and lovingly, with imagination and rigor, loving kindness and compassion. It is a scholar's greatest hope – that those who work beside and follow afterwards will surpass and enhance what already has been done. These two scholars exemplify that hope fulfilled. I have smiled the entire time we have worked on this project as I read their thoughtful prose . . . Most impressive is that they led the way in modeling how three authors might write together.
>
> (Carolyn Ellis in Adams *et al.*, 2014: location 97)

Introduction

This chapter is structured differently from the other chapters in that although there will be some analysis, the full analysis of this particular autoethnography will come in the following, concluding chapter. I want readers to digest this story fully and because it deals with sensitive issues,[1] I want to provide as many details as possible to the reader. From my point of view as a feminist autoethnographer, it should demonstrate that not all feminisms are the same and not all feminists respond similarly. I want the reader to make his or her own judgements on these matters and, as I say, I will offer my analysis in the following chapter 'Sensitizing the feminist 'I''.

My sad story begins . . .

8 January 2010

Room 209 at my department's building.

I am at the podium lecturing in front of my 3rd year undergraduate class, Family, Gender & Society. The students are always very attentive and I notice Karen, one of my brightest students, is smiling as she listens to me speaking. Today the lecture is on postmodern families. I am comfortable in myself and I continue, '*We take up the theme of the postmodern family as outlined in the 1990s by Giddens, Bauman and the German sociologists Ulrich Beck and Elizabeth Beck-Gernsheim. Their approaches contend that the family is being basically restructured as a result of more individualised lifestyles, changes in the nature of emotions and modes of living. In this view, the family has not disappeared or entered crisis but is being shaped by new kinds of politics'*. As I am speaking, I look around the room and see that Emily is wanting to ask a question. Her hand is up. I stop talking and say, *'Yes, Emily, please what would you like to say?'* Emily responds enthusiastically and the other students shake their heads – at what I am not sure. Emily continues, *'I've read the sociologist, Carol Smart's,* Personal Lives *and as a feminist she tends to be critical of this view of the family and sees the family as a versatile and diverse form but I want to know how we can best define the concept, family or is it families nowadays? When and where was it first defined sociologically?'* '*Yes*', I say, '*I agree with Carol Smart*'. Just as I continue my answer to Emily's question, the house bell rings, signalling that my class is over. Students stand up and get ready to leave. Over the noise of this hustle and bustle, I raise my voice and say, *'Let's come back to Emily's question, Tuesday in the next class'*. Some students nod their heads, while others are heading already out the door to their next class. I think, *'Emily's is an excellent question'*.

3 pm, same day

My Family, Gender & Society class is over and I am walking to my office. I am thinking, *'The class went well'* but I keep pondering Emily's question, *'When and where was it first defined sociologically?'* I am thinking now about all the concepts I am using in this class. *'What a good question Emily asked'*. I have been teaching courses on gender and the family for 15 years and, more recently, this course, Family, Gender & Society. I notice increasingly that students do not know the origins of foundational concepts in this field and/or they tended to misuse these concepts. There has been a continual refrain in this class about the origins of concepts. I ask myself, *'Why don't I write a more general book clarifying these foundational concepts and their origins as well as establishing conversations between family scholars. Something like "Contemporary Family Issues"'*, I think enthusiastically. This would be very helpful for students grappling with these concepts. I am feeling excited at my new idea. I arrive at my office door, fiddle with my keys, unlock my door and walk in elated.

4 February 2010

My office in my department's building.

I have invited to a Skype meeting three American scholars, Ursula, Penelope and Ruth – all who I know well through my attendance at gender conferences in the US over the years. I am especially fond of Ursula because we have shared many conference experiences together; I have been an informal mentor for her and we have become friends. *'Maybe, I could continue mentoring her'*, I think, *'It is such a pleasant experience'*. Because I respect their work, I want to ask them if they would be interested in agreeing to co-author with me a book called *Contemporary Family Issues*, which would begin to answer some of the questions posed by my students and focus on key concepts in the field. These potential co-authors are all younger than me. I know they are solid young scholars and age does not matter to me. During this Skype meeting, everyone is keen to be involved in co-authoring my proposed book and we decide to contribute to the writing of a book proposal. I have already contacted a publisher, New Publisher, who is keen to receive the book proposal. We agree to send any additions of the book proposals to me by the end of May and, as lead author, I will make additions, revisions and send the final proposal to the publisher. I am the main organiser because I have had more experience than they have in writing book proposals. It is all very exciting and I am relieved that we have agreed to have a feminist thread throughout all our writing for this book. '*What luck*', I think, feeling contented.

15 May 2010

My home near the university.

I am in my 2nd floor study on my computer and I receive a message on my work answer phone from Carol, an editor at New Publisher. She says, '*After sending the book proposal to five reviewers, we want to take the book on. We will be sending you a contract very soon*'. I feel delighted because I see this book as a way of mentoring my co-authors – they do not have much experience publishing books. I send an email telling them the good news. Ursula responds '*Fantastic*'; Penelope writes, '*Wonderful*'; Ruth says, '*Many thanks for letting us know, this is excellent news*'.

1 June 2011 – 31 July 2012

In January 2011, I retire from my university post. This life transition to retirement is not as easy as I had anticipated and in the first few months I am somewhat depressed and anxious. It is hard for me not to see students and colleagues on a daily basis, although I left as Head of Department and don't miss that administrative part of my work. I decide to live in Helsinki with my partner as well as in our Cornwall home in Truro, UK. I divide my time between both places, although I am officially resident in the UK. I continue to write my contributions to *Contemporary Family Issues*. Soon after I retire, Ruth one of my co-authors writes an email to all of the co-authors to say that she has to leave the project for personal reasons. Basically, Ruth has no time to do the writing for our book. In June, Penelope writes an email to Ursula and me asking if she can approach another scholar from the US, Helga, to take Ruth's place. Ursula and I agree. Very soon afterwards, Penelope tell us enthusiastically that Helga is '*eager to take Ruth's place*'. I think, '*All is in order and we can be on track to deliver the manuscript by August 2014*'.

28–31 October 2012, Escondido, California

My writing for *Contemporary Family Issues* takes a back seat when I have to travel to the US to visit my dear, dying mother. It was a traumatic experience for me and after she dies while holding my hand, I am left feeling vulnerable and grieving. In November, when I come back from Stateside, I get words of sympathy from

Penelope and Ursula. I sense that they will understand if I am delayed. I need to mourn. I was close to my mother and after many years, she accepted me as a lesbian. She said many wonderful things to me before she died and I have never forgotten those gifts of words.

2 December 2012

Our home in Helsinki, Finland – a Skype meeting with Ursula.

Still recovering from my mother's death, I feel sad but also feel that I want to reach out to someone and that someone is Ursula. I start, '*How about if we write our chapter on "living apart together" families jointly? I have been giving you lots of career and writing advice and I enjoy it very much*'. I remember that although I am older than Ursula, we seem to both benefit from our friendship. I also remember we spoke at a recent conference about how I was a good mentor for her and she was an excellent mentee for me. I continue, '*You have a wonderful writing style as I have read some of your work and we could work well together*'. Ursula, a little hesitant, says, '*That sounds great for me and yes, I think we could work well together too*'. I say, '*I am so much enjoying writing my chapters for* Contemporary Family Issues. *It feels as if I am writing some of my best work ever. I have been reading a lot and it has been a wonderfully enriching experience*'. Ursula says, '*Gosh I wish I could have time to do my chapter. It sounds like you have time and space; I guess that because you're retired*'. As I listen to what Ursula says, I feel a little sad that she has so little time to write. She is very busy. Quickly, I change the topic and ask, '*How is Joe (her child)*?' I am aware that I don't want to raise Ursula's envy about my writing.

30 May 2013

The book collaboration is going well because we are keeping to our timetable and writing schedules. As I told Ursula last December, I have been writing some of my best work ever and I am enjoying it very much. My co-authors and I agree to comment on each other's chapters. So far, two chapters have been circulated – Penelope's and Helga's. All my co-authors have been very busy with their university work and I am aware it is difficult for them to find time to write their chapters within the timescale, but they are writing and I am wanting to be encouraging. I have read through their chapters thoroughly and they are good because their chapters have a clear structure, are informative and scholarly. However, I notice almost at once while reading both Penelope's and Helga's chapters, that the feminist 'red line', so to speak, that we all agreed to include throughout all of our chapters appears to be 'faint', if not missing in their chapters. They have a very different writing tone from mine and I feel disappointed.

31 May 2013: a Skype meeting with Penelope, Ursula and Helga

I say (with a slightly apologetic tone) '*I like your chapters very much Penelope and Helga but I expected that your chapters would be more feminist orientated, as we* agreed. *I don't mean to be overly critical but some of your key concepts such as gift, exchange, kinship, etc., you define and the authors Morgan, Carsten and Levi Strauss you mention – both these concepts and these authors have been criticised from a feminist viewpoint already in the 1970s. My advice would be to include in your chapters a closer look at these concepts and authors through a feminist lens. I'll send you the key feminist references in an email so that you can include them. I think it is important as we agreed to offer a feminist focus'*. After I say this, there is a long silence and almost immediately, a change of topic when Ursula says, '*OK, Betsy we need to give the others a deadline on our living apart together chapter*'. I hear some heavy and perhaps, nervous breathing through my speakers. Immediately, I started to feel uncomfortable . . . '*Oh dear, what have I done*', I think to myself.

5 June 2013, 7 am

I am at my computer ready to begin reviewing the final draft of my chapter on family and embodiment. I want to send it off to my co-authors today. But I am not feeling so happy. I am anxious. As I start reading, I think of our last Skype meeting. I am aware that as a retired Emeritus Professor I have much more time for writing than my co-authors. I don't have any pressure to do this book. For me, it is fun. My tenure does not depend upon my writing this book or any other book for that matter. I don't have that worry anymore. But I have a gnawing sensation in my gut that there may be a conflict growing between me and my co-authors – a conflict between what we agreed on and their struggle to obtain tenure or indeed a permanent position in academia. There is a paradox here because career pressures are especially strong for women, and feminist academics are subjected to especially harsh double standards. Perhaps, my co-authors feel that they have to fight for their survival in some way. I honestly don't know and I feel too shy and maybe even afraid to ask them because they are not close friends. If this is a fight for survival, they may be more preoccupied with themselves and their careers and less able to adopt the perspective of the other – me[2] – an older feminist with a long list of book publications. Maybe all of this is a factor as to why the feminist lens was missing from Penelope's and Helga's chapter, I think. '*Was I too harsh in my criticism of their chapters? Why did they not want to emphasize the feminist focus as we had agreed? What are the larger issues at play for them? Are they afraid? Their lived work lives are very different from mine. I don't really have a proper, paid work life anymore. Surely, they have the pressure to publish more and faster*'. I play with the strap of my wristwatch – pulling it up and down and then, when I stop, I tie my hair behind my head. I look out the window and see the sun is shining and it reflects back on the water near the harbour. It is a glorious day in Helsinki. But, inside here in my study I am struggling to find more of what I am feeling. I am not comfortable. I am myself feeling afraid. '*Oh dear, did I hurt them?*', I ask myself. '*I sincerely hope not*'. I think, '*Maybe I should have been more sensitive to them. Helga is new to the collaboration. Maybe, she is unaware of the agreed feminist focus. Oh, but Penelope would surely tell her that*'. The thought keeps coming back to me that something labelled 'feminist' for them as non-tenured academics could potentially jeopardize a tenure case at some institutions. '*Is this true for them?*', I ask myself and think, '*Their living in the third wave is not the same as for me coming from the second wave*'. I am still feeling uncomfortable and fearful. Why? I am not sure. '*They must respect my opinion*', I think tentatively.

10 am, same day

My chapter is completed and I send an email to my co-authors with my chapter attached. I want to be light, superficial and cheery and say, '*Hello, Ladies, Here is the first draft of Chapter 3 on embodiment. Comments welcome and look forward to seeing you on Skype. Betsy.*' After sending that email I send another email to Penelope and Helga that includes the feminist references I promised to send them for their chapters after I 'reviewed' their chapters.

28 June 2013

I am in Helsinki in our study at my computer. It is late afternoon. I adjust my chair and am feeling comfortable. I am waiting for a Skype group call with my co-authors. While waiting, I am thinking, '*I have sent in one of my completed chapters to them and I am very satisfied with the first draft. I see it as scholarly and of a very high standard, especially when I map out future research vis-à-vis family embodiment*'. I hear the familiar Skype ring tone and the conversation begins with Penelope who says, '*I hope everyone is fine*'. I hear Ursula and Helga saying simultaneously, '*Yes I am*'. I chip in, '*Yes fine*'. Penelope continues, '*If I can begin . . . I've read through your chapter, Betsy . . . It is clear that the emphasis, order and style of the chapters Helga and I have written are different to yours. Our work presents an educational guide, where as your work offers a more critical perspective. Your work is more polemical and you raise issues that are not looked at by us*'. I am thinking, '*But my chapter is feminist orientated and of course, I can be nothing else but critical or political which we said we would do in the book proposal*'. For reasons, unknown to me, I am unable to speak. I feel numbness in my brain setting in. Penelope continues, '*This is not to be disapproving of the work you have done*'. I remain silent and immediately, I think, '*But, for myself, it sounds like you are doing just that – being critical and disparaging. Is this payback time for how I responded to you and Helga's chapters? No, it can't be. They would not do that*'. Ursula chips in, '*Yes, both Helga and I agree with Penelope*'. I think to myself, '*But, Ursula we are writing partners and I thought feminist friends, you know the style of my writing. Why are you chipping in?*' I am afraid to say this out loud. Helga says, '*Yes, that is true*'. Penelope continues, '*It is evident that you are rather perplexed by our comments, we are sad about this . . . We all write in diverse ways and that is OK. What we are talking about is the quality of your chapter rather than your different writing style . . . We found it difficult to follow the main points of your argument. You really need to narrow down the content of the chapter . . . our concern is that you make proclamations in your chapter that appear as unsupported and inadequately referenced – propelled by a set of postulations rather than being clearly reasoned . . .*'. I think to myself, '*Hang on. This chapter had 115 references and 15 footnotes, what are they talking about?*' Again, I am afraid to talk out loud what I am thinking because I feel outnumbered and can't even depend upon Ursula any more. I sit back and adjust my chair as I feel uncomfortable and too hot. I start to feel ashamed and think, '*Is my work so bad?*' Penelope continues, '*At certain points, you speak quite glibly about earlier work . . . If the book is to be worthwhile . . . we want to engage the readers – take them with us. Your work doesn't do that*'. Now, I am utterly speechless and feeling somewhat confused. I roll my eyes, as I know they can't see me. My Skype video is not working. For me, this is all happening so fast, I think, '*Try to compromise, Betsy, you don't want to lose them now*'. '*OK*', I say, '*I'll look at my chapters and get back to you with changes*'. There is a long pause. Then, Penelope says, '*There is one more issue which is about the idea of this book. It may have been your idea but you probably agree that the way the book has developed . . . was a result of mutual discussions. It has been a collaborative effort in which we have made equivalent inputs. So we agree and we hope you do too that no one person is the first author in terms of leading the authoring or thinking out of the book*'. I am thinking to myself, '*Wait a moment, I am the first author here, I invited you to be co-authors – not the other way around*'. I don't understand what is happening now. And because I feel offended, afraid and intimidated, I remain silent. Now, I am half listening. I hear in the background Penelope speaking, '*. . . Also because we see this as a co-authored book we all want to be happy with it in the end. And we are all agreeing that so far the manuscript is not yet of good enough to be published.*' Still in shock, I am thinking, '*Oh dear, this can't be happening. From my point of view, my work is as good as my co-authors. How can they say that about my writing? I am the one who secured the book contract. Do they see me as having gone by my sell-by date? Why isn't Ursula supporting me?*' I ask myself. She is just silent and agrees with the others. I thought of her as a friend and mentee. And I don't even know Helga well because she is Penelope's friend. Perhaps, she turned Penelope against me as things have changed a lot since Helga came into the writing group and Ruth left. I feel very, very sad and deeply disappointed. It has not yet sunk in what is happening. As I feel so despondent, I think, '*Maybe this is how it feels to be browbeaten. Is this bullying I ask myself?*' I don't know. I only feel bad.

29 June 2013

The next day, I go back to my chapter and make some revisions but I am aware that as I am making the changes my co-authors have asked for, I am taking out the strong bits of my work as well as the feminist focus. '*This is not right*', I think. I feel very sad and quite vulnerable – as if I am being harassed.

1 July 2013

I want to have a Skype conversation with Ursula and arrange a brief time to speak. But soon after our conversation starts, I sense that she is not supporting me.

Ursula tells me, '*Do all the changes they ask, Betsy. We don't want to hold up the book. The clock is ticking.*' I tell her that in my opinion it feels like I am being harassed even bullied by them and, when I do, there is silence from her end. We ring off and I feel worse than when the conversation began. I feel deep shame. '*That didn't help*', I think. The Skype conversations with my co-authors now stop because it is summer break. I send around another revised chapter. I decide to leave the strong bits in and not to follow my colleagues' advice by taking out the last section of my chapter, which to me is innovative. I know I am taking a risk. Surely, it can't as bad a piece of writing as they suggest.

During this time, I speak with my partner, Irmeli. She has been working very hard and we have not had much time during the last week to speak in depth about what is going on in our lives before we go to our summer cottage today. She has noticed that I have been very sad and I did say earlier in the week that I am having some problems with my new book.

While she is driving us to our summer cottage, Irmeli asks, '*What's happening with the book?*' I say, '*Well, not much at the moment as my co-authors appear to be very critical of my chapter on embodiment and see it as too political. To be honest, it feels as if I can't discuss with them anymore – or they want to put my work down. I feel my voice is being silenced. I think my work is good but they disagree.*' Irmeli responds, '*Betsy, this does not sound right. Why didn't you tell me sooner?*' I say almost crying, '*Well, I didn't want to tell anyone what was going on. At first, I thought they were right. I started to doubt myself and my work. I kept thinking my work was shitty, crap. I thought it was three scholars in agreement against one – little old me*'. Irmeli says excitedly, '*Don't be ridiculous. Your work is very good and you have published a lot of excellent feminist texts. I think you didn't tell me because it may be that you are being bullied. I don't know*'. She continues in her psychotherapeutic voice,[3] '*Very often when someone is being bullied, they don't tell anyone because they feel such deep shame*'. I burst into tears and Irmeli silently reaches out her hand to hold mine as she drives the car. As I squeeze her hand, I say with an almost inaudible sniffling, crying voice, '*You'll have an accident*'. Irmeli says laughing, '*Don't worry. I have an idea. Why don't you send your original book proposal and the chapter in question to some other colleagues? Ask their advice. How about George, Naomi and Diane, they are not only good colleagues but also established professors who know your work?*' '*Gosh*', I say, '*that is a brilliant idea. I'll do it when we get to the cottage.*' During the three hour ride to our summer cottage, I start feeling a little better. Still the shame is deep and won't shift inside me. I think, '*I need to check this out. I don't want to be belligerent. Irmeli's plan is a good plan as all three colleagues are specialists in my chapter's area. They will be honest with me and tell me if my work is not up to scratch or doesn't keep in line with the original book proposal*'.

When we arrive at the summer cottage, I have the resolve to write to my colleagues and do so after Irmeli and I have lunch. It is a sunny, warm day and the lake looks inviting but I bring out my computer. I start to write while Irmeli takes out the rowboat. I feel envious towards her, but know I will join her after

82   'She wrote it but look what she wrote'

I send these emails. I decide to send the same email to all three colleagues and it reads:

> *Hi . . .*
>
> *I hope all is well.*
>
> *Can you do me a HUGE favour?*
>
> *I am in the process of writing a book with 3 other colleagues (I attach the book proposal minus my co-authors' names). It is all about looking at conceptual heritages of various concepts used in family research. We trace the origins and how these can be applied today.*
>
> *To make a long story short my co-authors have described my work as either too 'political' or too 'polemical'. So I am asking you and two other colleagues to look this chapter over (it's still in draft form) and see what you think. Does it look like it won't fit into the book's scheme and are there any problems with it? I just really need outsides eyes as I am too close to it . . . We want to submit the final manuscript by the end of July.*
>
> *I hope you can do it and then write a few words what you think. Just be honest.*
>
> *It is a big favour I know but I have never had this experience before!*
>
> *Many thanks,*
>
> *Betsy*

After I send these emails with their attachments, I feel relieved. I just have to wait, I think to myself and go for a swim. Everything has happened so fast I am still in a state of shock and confusion, but the main feeling is shame.

11 July 2013

George (in an email sent to me):

> *I have now had a chance to read the chapter and also the outline of the book and to be honest I am not sure why your co-authors are so worried. Are they worried that a slightly more direct or could one say controversial chapter will affect sales, I would have thought the opposite. Also is it not the case that it is because of your name that others will buy the book.*
>
> *I found the chapter to be very useful as it provided me with a very full account of embodiment theory . . . Having said that, some of it was not immediately obvious or should I say immediately understandable only because of the fact that for me much of the literature is outside my knowledge. Also I suppose in some cases it was political although I am not sure that I would use the word polemical other than the fact that you were making an assertive and also*

'She wrote it but look what she wrote' 83

feminist argument. I also wondered, again given the topic, how the chapter could have been done in any other way given the fact that a good deal of the embodiment literature has been generated within a gender, feminist, class and ethnicity perspective. Having said that the question is: is it too political or polemical – I don't think so, but I have also read a lot of your work so I may be a little immune. Strangely enough I somehow expect a particular style/tone when I read your material, but that doesn't mean that it is polemical. I would define your style/tone as forceful and assertive, but that is what I expect.

On a slightly different front, but as a further support for the chapter, in the book outline it talks about the authors 'demonstrating the relevance of bold concepts to practice and applying them in an overtly political way to the here and now', isn't that what you are trying to do in your chapter. Therefore, I cannot see why the co-authors think that you have gone outside the parameters of the book outline. While I do not know the other authors, maybe they are less au fait with a particular style of sociological writing which is forceful and aiming to make a point, while nevertheless remaining within the realm of sociological/feminist thought. Actually if I think about it, although there is much of you within the choice of literature, there is much less of you within the commentary of the literature that you have assembled. This is especially true if you compare this paper with the one that you wrote for the special issue, where I felt that there was a good deal of your own personal politics within it. Personally that is why I think that it is very important.

Finally, I wonder to what extent your chapter seems more political or polemical in comparison with the topics of many of the other chapters, which at least from their titles appear a little standard and dry, for example culture, meaning and practice; ritual, belief and spirituality and finally kinship blood and communities. These chapters would not appear to be obviously earth-shattering, how many other pieces have been written on these issues although not necessarily within the contemporary families issues framework. Your chapter, in comparison, is controversial because the latest theoretical literature on embodiment is also controversial, at least in the sense that it is wanting to stir the accepted assumptions of the reader. Your chapter also does that because you are bringing those perspectives to your readership and maybe many of your readers have never dealt with the writings of Braidotti; Mamo; Murphy etc.

14 July 2013

Diane (in an email sent to me):

I've had a read of your very interesting chapter. To me personally, your objective to set out the lacuna surrounding the body within sociological thought and its trajectory of emergence into a sociology of the body drawing in and through feminist and other considerations of agentic self, identity, morality and so on seems quite clear and fits the remit of the book to engage and demonstrate a

84   'She wrote it but look what she wrote'

range of frames through which to interrogate the family. It seems to me that set up that way, the distinctions of anthropologically framed questions and sociologically framed questions are placed in implicit dialogue – which your introduction and conclusion could effectively parse. The text seems particularly useful for students at an honours level who are aiming to make sense of diverse traditions of thought surrounding family, gender and bodies.

Your chapter has considerable sweep and breadth, both theoretically and in terms of the empirical cases in point you bring up – but they work because you harness them to an argument for a mode of moral/empathetic interrogation (embodied ethics). I'm not sure I can see what the problem is for your colleagues. You could even pull the feminist theoretical point through further if you wanted to given that the early framing concepts of body-self you cover have informed trajectories feminist thought more broadly, even as the emergence of feminist politics/body analysis were contemporaneous with these theoretical moves and reciprocally informed them.

15 July 2013

Naomi (in an email sent to me):

I don't see the polemic in this chapter, which seems to be almost genealogical in tracing out the possible past conceptualizations of embodiment that might be sources for future conceptualizations. Your voice isn't taking on the tone of a manifesto, and there seems to be little cause for anyone to call this 'too political' unless they perhaps mean that *any* talk of embodiment might seem 'too political' in this moment when feminism enjoys what I believe Leila Rupp and Verta Taylor refer to as 'the doldrums' or 'abeyance'.

After I receive and read through these emails, I am relieved and feeling more confident. I had been at a real low, thinking my work was substandard . . . and these encouraging words cheer me up. I am happy to hear that my chapter is scholarly and will be acceptable in the academic community. I feel reassured. I decide not to send these reviews to my co-authors as I think it may only serve to provoke them. I sit back in my study chair. Still, I feel some shame inside me.

16 July 2013

We have returned to Helsinki from the summer cottage. I open my email box and receive an email signed by all three co-authors. The email starts by saying that they, all my co-authors, had a chat recently. Immediately, I think, '*So I am now being excluded, totally left out – are they meeting without me?*' I am feeling excluded and alone. I feel a wrenching in my stomach. I feel like I want to vomit. My co-authors tell me there is a '*basic disparity*' in orientation in the book and that they feel this cannot be resolved. They tell me that they '*respect my approach but it's not theirs*'.

Besides a different approach from mine, they have '*different views on collaboration and authorship*', etc. In the end, they tell me that they want to '*end our collaboration*', have me '*sign an Addendum to the contract*' to say that I will drop out of the collaboration and that they '*have spoken already with New Publishers to ask advice*' about how to go out about doing this. I notice that they would appreciate '*in good faith*' if I would leave the collaboration and sign the addendum. They are sad about how things have ended up (i.e '*We feel . . . sad about this, but feel it is the point to concur that we want very different things from the book*'). I think, '*Can this really be because I sent them my chapter without making their suggested changes?*'

As I read, I am still in a state of shock and I feel myself sadder and sadder. I am offended and sense that the 40 years of my academic training and success are being cancelled out. I am wondering, '*How could they do all this behind my back? Going to New Publishers without telling me? What was that about? Are they trying to besmirch my name to the publisher? Why would they do that? I don't believe we have a fundamental difference in orientation*'. Initially, I asked them – at least Penelope and Ursula – to be my co-authors because I wanted to work with them as solid, young, scholars? Perhaps things have changed since Helga joined the group. I think, '*Could she be behind this? I don't know. Was she envious of me because I have wanted to be a mentor?*' I am confused. I just don't know and it does not help speculating. '*But, I only wanted to help promote their career and mentor them on how to publish a book*', I ponder.

As I feel my face getting redder and redder, I continue reading the email and the words, '*in good faith*' hit my eyes. When I stop reading, I look blankly at the screen. I don't know what to do. I think, '*In all of my years, this has never happened to me before. I have published 13 books and 5 of them have been with co-authors. But having co-authors behave like this is a new experience for me. Consistently, my experiences with co-authors have been positive, indeed pleasurable. I sit slowly back in my chair. I thought I was being generous to these younger colleagues, but perhaps my initial criticism of their work as not having a feminist "red line" in May was too much for them. Yes, I was wrong. Although they didn't say anything at the time, I must have been wrong. I was out of line. They are of a different generation from me. The "F word" is perhaps too dangerous for them. But, I don't know, this all does not feel right*'. I am still confused as to their motivation for doing what they did. Maybe the simple reason is that I am now past my sell-by date so to speak. Perhaps, that is it. I don't know. Maybe it is that I am an old lesbian. '*Oh please don't go there, Betsy*', I tell myself. I stand up from my chair, take a long stretch and look out the window. It is raining – a typical summer downpour in Helsinki. The window is open so I smell the freshness of this cloudburst on the harbour street near my window. I'd love to be outside, not here in this study. '*I'd just wash these feelings away*', I think. I wish I was in one of those lovely sailing boats passing by my window in the Helsinki sound. I could almost feel the breeze on my face. '*At least I wouldn't be stuck in this room having to read this rather perplexing email on my computer*', I ponder. I sit back down. Now I am feeling desperate and ask myself, '*Is my work a piece of shit? It seems so*'. I feel tears fall down my face. I am crying and feel completely devastated.

17 July 2013

I am feeling anxious after having received that disturbing email of yesterday from my co-authors. I am wanting to get in touch with my New Publishers editor, Carol, who commissioned *Contemporary Family Issues*. I hope she can shed light on this matter and give advice as to what I can do. Perhaps she is as confused as I am as to what is going on with my co-authors. I ring Carol's assistant, Joe and find out that Carol is actually on holiday and after that at a conference abroad and won't be back for 3 weeks. I think, '*Oh dear, can I bear waiting?*' But I have no choice.

17 July – 10 August 2013

In the meantime, my feminist friends, including my partner, offer support. My beloved partner Irmeli says, '*You just have to wait now and I am sure the publisher will support you. You must remember that you have done nothing wrong. But, that is easy to say. I don't know whether or not you are being bullied, Betsy, but if you are it is hard to deal with. You need to start feeling better about yourself.*' At the same time, my dear friend, Diane tells me, '*I don't understand what your co-authors are trying to do, Betsy. In my opinion, I see it as really mean. Your work is always of a high standard. I don't understand their motivation. Perhaps, they want the book for themselves even though the idea for the book was yours. Maybe I am being too judgemental. I don't know what to say*'.

11 August 2013, 9 am

I decide to send an email to my editor at New Publishers, Carol, as I know she must be back by now. I ask her if we can speak on the phone anytime between 10.00 and 16.00 UK time and that I look forward to hearing from her.

11 August 2013, 3 pm

I hear the Marimba tone on my mobile. I answer, '*Hello, Elizabeth Ettorre*'. Carol responds, '*Oh, hi Elizabeth, it is Carol from New Publishers, you wanted to speak with me about the progress of* Contemporary Family Issues. *I understand from my assistant Joe, that there have been some issues recently*'. I say, '*Yes, my co-authors would like me to leave the collaboration as they have a problem with my work.*' Carol says, '*Well in all my 25 years of publishing, I have not come across this before. In my opinion, I see that your co-authors have decided to gang up on you. I see you as lead author and don't see how you can leave the collaboration. I understood the idea for the book was yours and I encouraged you to submit the book proposal when we first were in contact*'. Trying to be compromising, I say, '*Yes that is correct, but I don't mind if we go in alphabetical order for the book's authorship.*' Carol responds quickly, '*Wait a moment. I don't agree to that. You are lead author. Your name is known not your co-authors. The first I heard of them was when you told me they were your co-authors. You have to be lead author. We want the book to sell*'. I feel a sigh of relief as Carol is supporting me.

Carol continues, '*How about this? You write an email saying what we talked about and that you try to extract from them in the nicest possible way a submission date for the manuscript. I know that the book is nearly completed so that would be what we at New Publishers want*'.

I say, '*OK, I'll do that and copy both you and Joe into it*'. I have a slight pause and feel anxious saying, '*I should warn you, Carol, I am not sure that this will work. I have a feeling that my co-authors have made up their minds about not wanting to work with me any longer*'.

Carol says quickly, '*Well you must try. Think of this. Your co-authors came to New Publishers behind your back. So in my opinion, they are untrustworthy. But still, the book is nearly done and all we want is a submission date and we can deal with it from there. You don't have to have much contact with them after the date is agreed. We can handle that from our side. I am sorry I need to go now*'. '*OK*', I say, '*thank you very much for your help, Carol. I'll be in touch*'. I switch my phone off. Immediately, I am anxious but go to my computer to start composing an email to my co-authors. I still feel doubtful but am happy to have Carol's encouragement. '*Maybe the end is in sight*', I think, '*I want so much to get this book done*'.

6 pm, same day

I am having a telephone conversation with my old friend, Madeline, who is a feminist academic I have known for 40 years. After I apologise about having a rant about what is happening about the book, Madeline says, '*Betsy, I'm horrified. You have every reason to "rant", though it's scarcely that. In my opinion, it's all unbelievably crass, disrespectful and arrogant, not to say hurtful. And even worse if anxiousness around feminism is at root. I'm really pleased that Carol at New Publishers is backing you. I hope you get something sorted out that satisfies you and puts the pipsqueaks back in their boxes. Let me know how it progresses*'.

After speaking with Madeline, I am feeling more hopeful, but still the shame won't go away.

13 August 2013

Soon after, I send an email to my co-authors. In it, I apologise for the delay. I tell them that Carol, our Editor at New Publishers and I had a discussion on the progress of the book. She says that New Publishers sees the book as '*strong, measuring up to its foundational aims*' and that '*no author can be removed from the project in the last hour*' because each author's contribution is fully embedded into and across the fabric of the manuscript, etc. I mention also that regardless of any '*collaborator squabbles*', removing any author would be '*unrealistic*'. I said that Carol concurs and added that '*it would be impossible to extract any author's contribution at this stage*'. I tell them that the publisher notes that all authors have '*equal rights to copy editing of the manuscript*' and that Carol wants it to be known that from the start and since the contract signing stage, the view of New Publishers has been that '*I am lead author and that as a known Senior scholar in the field, I would help to draw readers to the text'. I also say that Carol asked me to write to them to consider '*a delivery date which is New Publisher's main concern*' because they want to begin planning for and organising production, marketing, etc. of the book. I also say that I hope we can progress with the book; that they would respond to this email and suggest a delivery date to New Publishers, cc'ing both Carol and Joe into their responses.

I feel relieved and yet a little bit afraid as to what my co-authors response will be. After Irmeli comes back from work in the early evening, I tell her what I have done. She says, '*Don't worry, Betsy. You have taken the Publisher's advice and now you just have to wait. Remember, you have done nothing wrong!*'

15 August 2013

I wake up early and open my email box to find an email addressed to myself (as Elizabeth not Betsy), Carol and Joe. This time the email comes from Ursula's email address and not Penelope's. The email starts by saying my co-authors have discussed my email (i.e. '*We have discussed your email from August 13th*') and that the book has stalled because we have not been able to resolve fundamental differences between us and '*that these differences are not just "minor squabbles"*' but substantial or foundational differences about the progress of the book.

I think, '*How interesting, a project stalling. I am bemused. I did not stall it. My opinion is that they did. They are talking about foundational differences. What is that about?*' I am confused. I invited them to this project and it was my idea to focus on key or core concepts. In my mind, the differences between us are because I want to express my feminist principles in my writing and for some reason, they don't want to or can't for whatever career reason.

'*Wait a minute*', I say to myself, '*Betsy, remember the fact that something labelled "feminist" for someone non-tenured could potentially jeopardize them is a real concern for them. I lived in the second wave and they did not*'.

As I read on, my co-authors talk about '*a significant difference*' in the '*quality of chapters*' and their '*general consistency*'. I push the hair from my forehead and ponder, '*Oh dear, are they now besmirching my scholarship and writing ability in front of Carol and Joe?*' I feel like I don't want to read on but I force myself, and again the shame starts to rise from within. I continue to read.

They say that my chapters are very different from theirs – that mine differs in '*its quality and form*'. . . . I think, '*Yes, my chapters are solidly feminist*'. I don't want to visit that issue again. I feel deep disappointment. I think, '*Perhaps, Madeline is right. Are they pipsqueaks that need to be put back in their boxes?*' But, '*I want to be as feminist as is possible. How can I help this situation when they all seem to be against me?*'

I read on. They say that although they have given feedback to me, '*no changes have been made*'. Their concerns revolve around any future critique concerning '*a non-coherent book with chapters that do not fit together*'. To my amazement, they make a sidebar to Carol and Joe asking them to confirm that the book will '*go out to external review*' and, if so, this will help to '*alleviate their concerns*'. '*What concerns?*' I think as I read, '*I don't understand why am I not included in this sidebar, so to speak. Why is it not – Carol, Joe and Betsy. Of course, they appear now to want distance by referring to me as Elizabeth? Can't they speak to me directly?*' I feel myself choking back the tears. I read on reluctantly not knowing what other affronts may follow. They go on to say that in the beginning of the project when authorship was discussed, my position was due to '*the first letter of my surname*'. I am thinking, '*We never discussed authorship as I just presumed I would go first. I guess I was wrong. But, I also remember I am willing to negotiate to put whoever does the most writing to go first*'. I read that they say (and remember this is my friend Ursula speaking for the others) that '*I have been the main contact with New Publishers but that I have assumed no senior or mentoring role or responsibility*' for conceptualising the book structure or content. I think, '*Oh dear, I initiated the project. The book was my idea. I invited them to join the project. What is happening?*' I feel a knot in my stomach and again the shame wells up. They go on to say that while Helga with a surname ending in C replaced Ruth, it is fitting to revisit discussions around '*author order*'. I am gobsmacked. '*Yes*', I am thinking, '*a lot changed since Helga entered the equation. Could she behind what is, in my opinion, this mutiny? At least Ruth would not have let this happen or behaved like this – or would she?*' I find it hard to read on, but I force myself and learn that my co-authors envisage that (for me, '*surprise, surprise!*') the '*most appropriate first author should be Penelope*' who they say thought up '*the foundational premise*' and book focus on '*conceptual legacies*', and her work thus far is '*most important*' in determining the book structure. I feel overwhelmed and am thinking, '*Yes, we did decide to look at the idea of conceptual legacies and it was an idea from Penelope. But, this idea emerged from my original idea to investigate how concepts have emerged in the field and that was my idea right from the beginning*'. Also, Ursula and I at a Skype meeting worked out the order of the chapters, not Penelope. It was a need that arose from the first moment Emily asked her question in my Family, Gender & Society class. I am thinking, '*That's why I wanted to organise this book – for my students not for myself or my career*'.

Oh dear, I see another side bar to Carol and Joe (minus me). In this side bar, they are asking advice about authorship and say that '*seniority should not determine authorship order*' (which of course I agree, but not in this instance). They also go on to say that in light of the intended readers as well as the '*philosophical differences*' amongst us, having '*Betsy as first author could give a confusing impression*'. They feel this impression would '*not reflect correctly*' the book's content. I am already getting a headache. I read on and see that they would like all of their concerns dealt with. Only then, will they agree to continue with the book. Basically, they want resolution of the problems and see if these problems aren't solved, they will be '*in a difficult place for forthcoming publication*'.

I stop reading and ask myself, '*What are they talking about – my giving a misleading impression? How would my name first give a wrong impression? Why are they not talking to me? I am part of this conversation. Are they using power in a subtle way? Are they trying to silence me?*' I feel sad and soon sick to my stomach, but I need to press on. Their email ends with a thank you to Carol and Joe in expectation of their advice. '*What about me?*' I think. '*I took the trouble to write to you folks. I secured the contract. This has not been easy for me*'.

I sit back in my chair feeling shattered. '*I am no good*', I think, '*past my sell-by date for sure. My work is crap, shitty. I can't even hold together this collaborative project. They are right my writing doesn't work anymore. Feminism is a "has been" like me*'. I feel deep shame.

17 August 2013

I contact Joe by email and ask him if there is any possibility of talking with Carol about my co-authors' recent email. He tells me that Carol has gone abroad again but will be back at the end of August/early September. He also says in the meantime New Publishers want to organise a Skype conversation with myself and my co-authors. However, nothing materializes.

15 September 2013

I return to the UK in September 2013. In mid-September, I hear that I am the recipient of the prestigious Emeritus Leverhulme Fellowship, which means I will need to go abroad to do some research. I am absolutely delighted and think, '*Maybe, my work is not that bad*'.

21 September 2013

I receive an email from Carol at New Publishers in which she says that it is going to be impossible to Skype in the next three days because my co-authors are not available. She wants my phone number so she can phone me on Thursday at 10 am.

26 September 2013, 10 am

I hear the Marimba tone on my mobile. I answer, '*Hello, Elizabeth Ettorre here*'. Carol responds, '*Hi Elizabeth, it's Carol. I wanted to tell you that your co-authors want to leave their contract with New Publishers. We will allow it and we very much want you to continue with the book either by yourself or with other co-authors*'. I am speechless and try to compose myself saying, '*Ohhhh, I did not know*'. Carol says, '*Well, we think it is best and please let me know if you will continue with the contract as we want you to*'. I respond, '*Yes, of course I would like to. Should I contact my co-authors any more or will you deal with it?*' Carol continues emphatically, '*No, I suggest that you have nothing more to do with your former co-authors. In my opinion, they have proved themselves untrustworthy and just keep your distance*'. '*Oh, OK*', I say hesitantly. '*I would still like* Contemporary Family Issues *to be a collaborative project. So it may take me time to get other co-authors*'. Carol says, '*Don't worry. Just let Joe and I know when you get other's agreement and we will proceed*'. '*Many thanks, Carol. I appreciate it*', I say. '*OK, I have to go now. Good luck*', Carol says and she signs off.

'*Wow*', I am thinking to myself, '*What happened? I guess my co-authors want to go it alone so to speak. But I still have the New Publisher contract*'. I feel relieved. I don't have to deal with my co-authors anymore – they are officially former co-authors.

29 October 2013

There is an email from Penelope, Ursula and Helga in my email box. Hesitantly, I open it. The gist of this email is that although they have left the collaboration, they want '*in good faith to be very clear on how they want to proceed*'. My eyes focus upon the words, in '*good faith*'. I think, '*What does "good faith" have to do with it? In my opinion, you proved yourselves as untrustworthy by going behind my back? Is that what you mean by "in good faith"?*' I read on and see that they plan to take their work on *Contemporary Family Issues* to another publisher and they want my assurance that I will not use any of their work as I continue with my New Publishers contract. They go through a very detailed analysis, chapter by chapter, of who owns what work and additionally who owns what versions of the Introduction chapter. They say that they '*hope that I am not insulted by their email*' (which, of course, I am). They defend themselves by saying that their '*suggestion's are made to make distinct "boundaries"*' between their work and mine, as well as to enable '*a level of confidence*' as we all proceed with different publications. They ask for '*a short email*' to show I agree to what they suggest. At the very end, they hope that this email '*finds me well*'. As I read those words, I laugh out loud, '*Wish me well and in good faith*'. I am confused. I think, '*How odd that they want to "wish me well" and be "in good faith" after all the destruction, in my opinion, that surrounds this book*'. '*OK, Betsy*', I say to myself, '*just be kind, they are young*'. I ask myself, '*Am I being patronising? Maybe – and no, I do not intend to respond to this email*'. Of course, I would not use their work. I have never plagiarised in all of my career. I am thinking, '*What is the point of their email? Why don't they just get on with it and leave me alone*'.

I contact my friend, Diane, tell her what has happened (re: about what I now refer to as '*the plagiarism email*') and ask her advice. She advises, '*Betsy don't answer it. In my opinion, they only want to make you feel bad or to win some kind of battle they started. As far as I am concerned, it does not appear as good faith; in my opinion, it is bad faith what they are doing. So just let it be and follow the publisher's advice. Don't have anything more to do with them. . .*'

18 November 2013

An email comes to my inbox from Penelope, Ursula and Helga. Basically, they are re-sending their 'plagiarism email' sent on 29 October. But this time, they are cc'ing a solicitor '*who has advised on the matter*'. Again, they ask for a '*short reply*'. After reading this, I feel deflated but notice luckily that the email includes the solicitor's email address. So, with advice from Irmeli and Diane, I compose and send an email to him. The email says that I am writing about '*the plagiarism email*' into which he was copied. (Of course, I don't refer to their email as 'the plagiarism email'). I tell him that I tried ringing him, I understand that he is quite busy. I also say that I left a message on his answer phone with my mobile number for him to ring me. Because we have not been in proper contact, I say '*to expedite matters I decide to write an email, explaining my position*'. I say that I don't understand why these researchers '*appear to be panicking*', as that is what their emails say to me. In academia, every scholar knows that '*we do not use another colleague's writing in one's own work – it would be plagiarism*'. Perhaps, I say, '*they are not familiar with plagiarism*'. Because I want to emphasize that I am experienced academic, I continue by telling him that '*I have written 13 books and have never plagiarised in my career and that I have been teaching about plagiarism for a number of years*'. I want him to know that I don't understand what their issue or problem is. I list three points or reasons why I have not responded to their emails and it goes something like:

1. I have been very busy working on a Leverhulme Emeritus Fellowship '*which involves a lot of international travel and I am often away from my computer*'.
2. '*I don't have any legal obligation to respond to their email*'. As far as I am concerned, '*the matter is closed. My last email sent to them was in mid-August 2013*'.
3. The publishers have advised me '*not to have anything more to do with them*'. I say something like, '*I don't know what Penelope, Ursula and Helga have been doing or said to my publishers but I have taken my publisher's advice seriously and I have not had anything more to do with them*'.

After listing these three points, I continue by saying that I am '*not totally happy to keep receiving emails from them*' and that as far as I am concerned, '*the matter is closed and was closed when they left my book contract*'. Because I don't want to receive any more emails from them, I say that in my opinion, '*I am starting to feel harassed by their emails*' and that I would be very happy for them not to contact me anymore. '*I ask him to pass on this message for me*'. The matter is closed. I no longer wish to receive emails from them. In the end, I ask him to confirm receipt of this email. The waiting for a response is difficult because I don't know what my co-authors have told him, but I will not contact them to ask.

24 November 2013, 9 am

I receive an email from the solicitor, which is very basic. He tells me he will inform my co-authors that I have contacted him. I feel a little deflated from his email, but I suppose a solicitor doesn't mince words.

12 noon, same day

A Skype call with my friend Diane.

I say excitedly to Diane, '*Can you imagine, my former co-authors approached a solicitor as a way of getting me to say I would not plagiarise their work?*' Diane says calmly with a hint of repugnance, '*Betsy, this is outrageous. You have done nothing wrong. In my opinion, your co-authors have wanted to damage your reputation with the publisher. Their motivation is not clear to me. Perhaps, they wanted the book for themselves*'. '*Oh, I don't think so*', I say. Diane continues, '*Remember we are academics and our whole career is based on our reputations. Maybe what they have done could be considered libellous. . . .*.[4] Based on my discussion with Diane I decide to investigate whether or not I should engage the help of a solicitor in a libel case. I write an email to my local solicitor who is a specialist in libel. I ask what the fees would be for a libel case and how best to proceed.

25 November 2013

I open my email box and I see I have a response from my local solicitor. I open it excitedly and in the email he thanks me for my enquiry, he would be '*happy to meet me to discuss a possible claim*' and can offer either '*a half hour consultation for £100 plus VAT with no written advice*' or a '*full hour consultation for £350 plus VAT with written advice*'. He says '*ongoing charges are calculated on a time taken basis, etc. and he looks forward to hearing from me*'.

I sit back in my chair and stare at the screen. '*Gosh this is expensive*', I say out loud to myself, '*I think I'll give this a miss*' and send a brief email to him to that effect.

27 November 2013

I am going to visit my friend Madeline (of '*pipsqueaks*' fame). When I arrive, she is eager to hear about how the book is progressing. I give her and her partner, Linda a blow-by-blow description of what has been happening, including my former co-authors' recent exchanges with a solicitor. Linda wants me to ring her solicitor friend, Mary, because she thinks that she may give advice over the phone for free. '*After all, the question is Betsy: are they besmirching your reputation with New Publishers?*', Linda asks at dinner that evening.

Linda is horrified at how I have been treated and, with the recent development of my former co-authors involving a solicitor, she is furious on my behalf. '*I don't think you are in the wrong here, Betsy. But no wonder you feel so badly*', she says with emotion. Madeline interjects, '*Yes, Mary is quite reasonable and would be able to help. She is a libel specialist*'. We talk about this over dinner and I decide that Linda will contact Mary on my behalf. While Madeline and I are in the kitchen cleaning up, I hear Linda in the sitting room. She is speaking to Mary. '*Betsy come here*', Linda shouts. I run to the sitting room with a towel and wet hands. I motion that I first need to dry my hands. I do and then Linda hands her mobile to me and says, '*Mary's on the line now*'. '*Oh, hello, Mary, this is Linda's and Madeline's friend, Betsy. Thank you for taking the time to try to help*', I say out of breath. Mary says, '*My pleasure, Betsy*'. Immediately I feel calm. Mary continues, '*Linda told me about what has happened with your book and in my opinion you may have a libel case. It may be that your co-authors have attempted to, whether consciously or not, damage your reputation with the publisher. I appreciate for academics you only have your reputation so this is not a small issue for you. But, I must warn you in Britain anyways, it is hard to prove libel without damaging your own reputation. All your dirty laundry gets washed in public, so to speak. That is the first factor and the second is finance. The litigations for these cases usually last a long time. Simply, they are quite expensive. The third factor is these cases inevitably get into* the national press. Can you bear it? So those are the issues you need to think about. It sounds like you still have a contract for the book. Your co-authors are now former co-authors and you can proceed with the book as you would want. It seems like New Publishers still trust you so your reputation is intact with them. The question is whether or not you are of the opinion that your former co-authors are capable of damage to your reputation in future. You could threaten a case and perhaps they will back down. But, I don't advise that line of action. Also, there is a slight problem as they live in the US and the libel or slander laws are different there. My advice would be to take no action. As I say, you have the book contract. Also, you are under no legal obligation to respond to any emails from them. They have nothing at the moment. So I'll leave it up to you'. I feel gratitude for her advice and say softly, 'Thank you very much for this advice, Mary. It has been very helpful'. As I say this, both Linda and Madeline look on – Madeline has a slightly worried face and Linda is smiling, anticipating my gratitude. I push the end button and pass the phone on to Linda as I say, 'Many thanks, that was very helpful. Mary suggests I don't proceed, but hinted if anything further happens, I could.'

28 November 2013 – 31 March 2014

During these months, I contact about 30 internationally known feminists in an attempt to engage them in co-authoring the book with me. By March, I get the agreement of four feminist scholars and I am delighted. They are enthusiastic. I contact New Publishers and tell them the good news. I also outline with my new co-authors an agreeable timetable. Things are looking up. New Publishers tell me that they need to have my former co-authors sign an addendum to the contract to release themselves from it. This means I can now move on with my new co-authors. Joe writes an email to my former co-authors asking them to sign an addendum which '*removes them officially from the contract*'. I am beginning to feel a huge burden lifting from my shoulders. However, this will be short lived as an email written to Joe (cc'd to me) arrives in my email box.

31 March 2014

The email is from my former co-authors and thanks Joe for his email; refers to '*the plagiarism email*' and the fact that it has not been responded to; says that they are '*happy to sign the addendum, in principle*'; they are pursuing a new contract with a new publisher and that they '*simply want to agree the borders between their work and mine*'. Lastly, they say that their email is sent '*in good faith*'. They acknowledge that they cc'd me in this email and want a response from me to their '*the plagiarism email*' prior to their '*signing the attached addendum*'. While reading this email, I feel sick to my stomach. '*Again, what is this about wishing me well?*', I ask myself. Maybe they really mean it, but in my opinion, it feels so gratuitously ingratiating. I ask myself, '*What are they doing?*' Come on . . . give me a break. The shame that I haven't felt for a few months is returning, welling up inside me. I start to feel devastated again.

1 April 2014

In order to deal with my co-authors' worry that I will use their work in my book, Joe writes an email to me asking me to look over a document that will terminate our agreement to do *Contemporary Family Issues*. The document is almost identical to '*the plagiarism email*' I received from my former co-authors on 29 October 2013. I read it over and start to feel uncomfortable. '*Something is not right*', I tell myself. I decide to make a Skype call to my friend, Diane who I now refer to jokingly as '*my consultant*'. When we meet on Skype, she says she is not surprised that my former co-authors are seeking another publisher. She reminds me that a few months ago she said that they wanted to take the book from me and I did not believe her. She says, '*Betsy, they won't sign the contract release form with New Publishers unless you say you won't plagiarise them. Joe at New Publisher is trying to ease the situation by sending you the document to terminate the agreement which basically states you agree to not use each other's work. There are many problems which I see emerging: (1) basically it appears as if your co-authors have now their own contract with their own book but don't want you to continue with New Publishers unless you say you won't plagiarize them; (2) it looks like they are engaging in a game of cat and mouse which is appalling and unprofessional – you sign; we sign; you don't sign; we don't sign. In my opinion, they have you over a barrel Betsy and I don't like it. Again, in my opinion, I see this as unprofessional. You don't owe them anything, Betsy*'. She ends with a firm voice. '*OK*', I say, '*but what shall I do?*' I am feeling totally vulnerable and powerless, but glad that Diane is helping me. Diane says, '*Well, let's think for a moment. I remember you told me that so far you did not reply to any of their emails and Mary, that nice solicitor friend of Linda's, told you that you are under no legal obligation to respond to them and furthermore, said that you could have a libel case. I also remember Carol, your editor at New Publishers told you in your telephone conversation some time – was it last September – to have "nothing more to do with them". But, Betsy, the bottom line is that it goes without saying that* Contemporary Family Issues *with your new co-authors would not be utilising chapters which they, as former co-authors, wrote. You would never plagiarise their work. The irony is that the book was your idea. It could be argued that they have taken your idea for themselves. This really is a mess and New Publishers are trying to help. But my advice would be that you don't sign the agreement New Publishers sent. It is not only that you have never plagiarised — but, Betsy, authors are not customarily asked to sign off on additional legal undertakings on this basis. Your book contract with New Publishers has a provision already that stipulates to original work belonging to the author/s being what is submitted. Thus, the agreement is both redundant and impugns your professionalism. I wouldn't do it. And I advise you not to*'.

I am listening very carefully and taking notes as Diane speaks. There is a long pause and then I say, '*Wow, this is so complicated but I see what you mean. You've said all along that this is not my fault and I have done nothing wrong. Perhaps, I need to now go elsewhere and leave the New Publisher's contract for good*'. Diane says, '*That may be the best way forward, Betsy. Start afresh. Hey, I have to go now*'. I say, '*OK. A million thanks for your help. I'll keep you posted*'.

I am in my study and feeling defeated, but somehow hopeful. I start composing an email to New Publishers with Diane's notes incorporated into it. I write that I have never plagiarised and that authors are not customarily asked to sign off on additional legal undertakings on this basis. I also write that my book contract with New Publishers already has a provision that stipulates original work belonging to the author/s is submitted. Thus, the agreement is both redundant and impugns my professionalism.

I feel quite sad as I write. I am aware New Publishers are not at fault. They have been very helpful, but I keep hearing a refrain in my mind that Carol said 6 months ago on the phone to me, *'Well in all my 25 years of publishing, I have not come across this before'*. *'Well in all my 25 years of publishing, I have not come across this before'*. *'Well in all my 25 years of publishing, I have not come across this before'*. *'Well in all my 25 years of publishing, I have not come across this before'*. *'Well in all my 25 years of publishing, I have not come across this before . . .'*

'Me neither', I think as the refrain goes on in my head. I feel those tears welling up again.

I send my email to Joe and Carol with the ending, *'To be honest, if the book is not able to go ahead with myself as the lead author and the new co-authors writing their agreed chapters, I would like to end my collaboration with New Publishers and withdraw* Contemporary Family Issues *as a New Publisher's title'*. I tell them that my intention would be to seek a new publisher who will take the book as it is. I'd be most grateful if they would let me know what New Publisher decides because *'I am eager to move from a challenging and time consuming experience'*. After I post my email to New Publishers, I feel very sad but still hopeful. I need a new start with this book – a fresh start. That may mean a new publisher, I think.

3 April 2014

Two days later I receive an email from Joe which is lovely and warm, but sad. Joe tells me that he is sorry for *'the amount of frustration'* all of this has caused me. He says that this whole matter is *'unusual for New Publishers'* and that after talking with Carol, they think it might be best for me *'to take the project to another publisher'*. They are able to cancel the whole project and *'have attached a document which does that'*. They also ask for me *'to return half of my advance (£60.00)'*. At the end, Joe reiterates that he is *'really sorry that this project hasn't worked out'* and he *'wishes me all the best for the future'*. After I read this email, I feel very sad. *'Why does it have to be this way?'*, I ask myself. *'Well now I can go to another publisher and I don't have to have anything more to do with my former co-authors. I can focus on a new book, with new co-authors'*, I think. Within the next hour, I sign the contract release form for New Publishers and pay back my £60 advance fee. I write to all my new co-authors to tell them in a nutshell what has happened (i.e *'My former co-authors who left the project will not sign a contract release form unless I sign a legal contract saying that I will not use their work in our current book . . . To make a long story short I would like us to take the book elsewhere and I have asked to be released from the New Publisher contract and they have agreed. So now I am writing to ask if you would agree to my including you and your chapters in a revised book proposal of the same name . . . Please let me know if you would be willing to continue on this project asap*') and I prepare the former book proposal for a new submission. I am happy that I already have my new co-authors CVs, addresses, etc. that I can send out, but first I wait for their permission to resubmit our proposal to a new publisher.

10 April 2014

Within days I hear from all my co-authors who agree to stay with the project. I send the proposal and additional needed material, including a sample chapter (i.e. my highly criticized one, criticized by my former co-authors) on embodiment to New Horizons Publishers.

16 April 2014

Within a week, I hear from an Editorial Assistant at New Horizons, Paul ('*Oh, the local, Joe*', I think) by email. He tells me that they had an internal review process and will send the proposal out for peer review and get back to me in 2–3 weeks. After I read this email, I am ecstatic and tense at the same time. I twist my hair behind my head and stand up abruptly. The waiting is almost too much for me. I hope they accept it, I think, '*It's just a case of waiting now. I'll be a nervous wreck*'.

14 May 2014

I see there is an unfamiliar email in my box from New Horizons. I quickly open it up. It is from Mary at New Horizons. The email is upbeat and includes a positive peer review of *Contemporary Family Issues*, which Mary '*is very pleased*' to be able to share. She says that the review is '*very encouraging – it finds the proposal ambitious and original*'. She very much '*welcomes my response to the review*' and says that the proposed book '*would fit beautifully on my programme . . . would have a strong chance of having a long shelf life*'.

'*Oh, another Mary*', I think. '*Wow this is great!*' As I quickly open up the review, my eyes immediately lock onto the words 'level of scholarship' and I read, '*Judging by the sample chapter the scholarship will be of a very high level*'. I keep looking at this sentence. I am dumbfounded, thinking, '*How can that be? All this time feeling shame that my work is not up to scratch and now this*'. '*Why?*' I ponder, '*Was it good all along? How could it be? It was crap! But I hardly changed anything after my former colleagues implied my work, particularly this chapter, was substandard and not well referenced. How can this be? Scholarship of a very high level!*' I sit back in my study chair and feel a sigh of relief – I think, '*This story is not only mine, it is co-owned with all those women, people whose voices have been shamed, shunned and silenced*'.

As we saw in the epigraph that began this chapter, a scholar's greatest hope is to work with those whose research '*will enhance what already has been done*' and who '*work hard and efficiently, challengingly and lovingly, with imagination and rigor, loving kindness and compassion*'. I've learned a big lesson from this experience – working with other scholars varies. It can be placed on a spectrum from pleasurable to not so pleasurable. It is the responsibility of us as scholars to deal with our own feelings that emerge from our collaborations, pleasurable or not. Although these feelings may define our subjective realities, these feelings don't define others' realities and their situations. I may be wrong in my opinions of others and what they do, but I feel I am right for myself – my feminist 'I'.

Notes

1 In writing this autoethnographic story, I had the feminist concerns of ethics and care foremost in my mind. I kept thinking, 'What should I do about these concerns in my story?' For most, if not all, of my autoethnographies, I have sought some sort of approval/recognition from all those in my story. For this story, I had a number of options and was not sure what to do. The options were (1) do nothing, just publish this story; (2) seek my co-authors approval prior to publishing my story; (3) send my story to them after I have written my story; (4) camouflage my story so no one will not know their identities (my co-authors and two others will; therefore, I consistently protect their identities and keep these highly confidential. Only two people – Diane, my 'consultant', and Irmeli, my partner – know their real identities); and (5) ask them to contribute their viewpoints to the story (they probably won't, and/or it could inflame my situation with them further.) At first, I was unsure what I would do. But after much thought, I considered ethically the best way forward as option 4 – camouflage my story no one will know their identities. I am very grateful to Carolyn Ellis who suggested these options and discussed them with me.
2 Many thanks for Maya Maor for pointing this out to me.
3 She is a psychoanalytic psychotherapist.
4 In the meantime, I read about UK libel/defamation laws on an 'Instructions for Authors', which is on my computer from a recent book I was involved in which says: '*Defamation is . . . a statement concerning any person which exposes him to hatred, ridicule or contempt, or which causes him to be shunned or avoided, or which has a tendency to injure him in his office, profession or trade*'. '*A publication to a third party of matter which in all the circumstances would be likely to lower a person's reputation in the eyes of right-thinking members of society generally*' (From Taylor & Francis Books Instruction to Authors © 2013 Taylor & Francis, 2 Park Square, Milton Park, Abingdon, Oxon, UK, OX14 4RN, p. 30). After reading this, I think Diane may be correct. I ask, '*Have I been injured in my profession by what has happened?*' I am not sure. I lost a book contract and in my opinion, some doggy emails were sent to my first publisher by my co-authors. '*Did these lower my reputation in the eyes of others?*' I answer, '*I don't know*' and think, '*For now, I will do nothing further*'.

References

Adams, T. E., Holman Jones, S. and Ellis, C. (2014) *Autoethnography: Understanding Qualitative Research*. Oxford: Oxford University Press (Kindle edition).

5 Sensitizing the feminist 'I'

> *The failure of this century is a failure of love ... What are we being called to do, what are we really made of, each of us alive on this planet today? What kind of love, what depth of love, what fierceness and searing love is required? Not a naïve, sentimental neoliberal love, but an unrelenting selfless love. A love that would vanquish systems built on the exploitation of multitudes for the benefit of the few ... A love that found value in our connection rather than in our competing ...*
>
> (Ensler, 2015: 4)

In this chapter, I want to reflect on the stories presented in the previous chapters of this book and I focus my attention and analyses primarily on Chapter 4: '*She wrote it but look what she wrote*'. I look at that chapter and others through a feminist lens. As I analyse this chapter alongside others, I use the criteria on the four ways in which I see autoethnography as a feminist method that I developed in the introductory chapter, 'Autoethnography as a feminist method'. At the end of the chapter, I will make some comments on autoethnography as critical feminist ethnography, look briefly at the politics of autoethnography *vis-à-vis* an 'ethnographic attitude' and suggest a way forward for feminists.

In Allen and Piercy's (2005: 159) important work, they contend that feminist autoethnography is 'the explicit reflection on one's personal experience to break the outside circle of conventional social science and confront, court and coax that aching pain or haunting memory that one does not understand about one's experience'. They argue further that feminist autoethnography

> is ideally suited for investigating hidden or sensitive topics ... about which little is known ... (it is) useful, regardless of the epistemological paradigm in which one works (because) feminists are adept at blending categories ... we do not have to be locked into a rigid adherence to relativism or foundationalism.
>
> (Allen and Piercy, 2005: 163)

What struck me about their work is their declaration of a fresh sense of empowerment, while they contend that the vulnerability feminist autoethnography uncovers is 'returned for strength' in a research approach 'grounded in humility' (2005: 156).

For them, feminist autoethnography involves 'a healing process' and the 'discipline of daily writing practice' helps the autoethnographer 'not to rush to judgement over any idea, feeling, emotion or sensation that emerges' (2005: 162). In a related context, Jewkes (2011: 63) contends that emotions are an intellectual resource in her autoethnography. Furthermore, she says that 'a more frank acknowledgment of the convergence of subject–object roles does not necessarily threaten the validity of social science, or at least, it is a threat with a corresponding gain'. From my point of view that gain is a sense of authenticity about myself and my story. Indeed, Carolyn Ellis (2004: 124) writes that our autoethnographic work seeks verisimilitude, as I mentioned earlier in Chapters 2 and 3. For her, autoethnographic research seeks generalizability not just from the respondents but also from the readers (2004: 195) and opens up rather than closes down conversation (2004: 22). This is a key response to autoethnography – an openness to listening to others – their behaviours and feelings and to oneself – one's emotions and relationships to these others.

In the Introductory chapter, I mentioned that feminist autoethnographers need to actively merge art and science and that this amalgamation is essential. I have already discussed that autoethnography is evaluated through the lens of science and art and that autoethnography bridges the gap between scientific and literary writing. When I started doing autoethnography, it was difficult for me to imagine that art is involved because I am schooled in the academic tradition of doing science, albeit social science. However, my feminism is always a moderating factor in my work and I listen to myself more as a feminist than as a 'social scientist'. Gradually, I find myself writing autoethnographies as 'artistic enterprises' that are emotionally charged. I find Allen and Piercy's, Jewkes's and Ellis's ideas all convincing. Their contentions provide me with the political rationale, hope and encouragement that I need to write this chapter. While all my stories in this book present sensitive topics, Chapter 4 '*She wrote it but look what she wrote*' is my most recent story, as well as the most difficult one for me to write. It is a delicate story in that I need to analyse it sympathetically. This story reveals how, in my opinion, an older, retired feminist can be bullied by junior colleagues – a hidden topic in the academic world. Writing that chapter demands from me a deep, agonizing sense of self-reflexivity. I am continually aware that 'This story is not only mine – it is somehow co-owned with my co-authors and all involved'. At the very least, ethically I need to try to represent these scholars in the most humane ways possible.[1] This is very difficult because for a long time – at least two years – I felt angry and hurt by my co-authors' actions. But, at the same time, few people are all evil, malicious, manipulative or incompetent. As a consequence, because my end goal is to use autoethnography as a feminist method, I need to ensure that the feminist concerns of ethics and care occupy a central place in my story and I need to show kindness, if not understanding to these younger[2] feminist colleagues.

I contemplate now that 'It is not easy to write this final or concluding chapter'. Just when I think, '*Nothing untoward now will happen to me as a retired academic in my career*'; just when I think, '*I'm somehow protected from belittling by my age and experience*'; just when I think, '*I will receive respect from my co-authors after many years of my being an active feminist scholar*' and just when I feel, '*These

colleagues, as co-authors and perhaps, feminists, would like me to mentor them' ...
It happens – I feel as if I am viewed as a has-been,[3] a woman academic past 'my sell by date', an outdated feminist scholar or a retired researcher, occupying the lowest 'chair' on the hierarchy of feminist researchers.

This is why my story, '*She wrote it but look what she wrote*' is such a shock for me and causes me a sense of devastation. I embody unworthiness and feel unappreciated. I find that there is no feminist utopia (although I do not believe in one) and that the 'feminist good life' is no safe haven for women as long as women are not totally equal to men. The most important thing for me in writing Chapter 4 is that I am reflexive, sensitive, open to my own foibles and humble. Although it is true that the feminist concerns of ethics and care occupy a central place in this previous chapter, autoethnography helps me to move beyond rigid definitions of what happens. My autoethnography privileges 'multivocality', providing 'representational space for the plural and sometimes, 'contradictory narrative voices' located within me as the researcher; provoking a deeper 'understanding of the often silent tensions that lie underneath the (misunderstood, perhaps,) behaviours' of my co-authors that I observe and 'focusing on the interaction' between me and my co-authors in my story (Mizzi, 2010: 2). In a related feminist context, Macdonald (2013: 134) uses a similar term, 'polyvocality'. He contends that autoethnography 'encourages polyvocality' and 'is vital with trans theory' because it 'implies the telling of multiple trans stories', not only the 'wrong body discourses' (2013: 134).

Autoethnography creates transitional, intermediate spaces, inhabiting the crossroads or borderlands of embodied emotions

In my story, '*She wrote it but look what she wrote*', I am occupying squarely an in between space – a space between feminist generations – older and newer – me being from an older generation and, in my opinion, my co-authors being from a more recent generation of feminists; a space between theory and practice (because I see my writing as a commitment to both); a space between public and private (because my story joins my needs as an intellectual with my love of writing) and a space between being willing and wilful (see Ahmed, 2014: 1209). Although eager to write critically, I am regarded as deeply wayward. As what I see as rancour between me and my co-authors escalates, I feel that I am nothing more than intransigent:

> ... *your work offers a more critical perspective* ... *Your work is more polemical and you raise issues that are not looked at by us.*

Therefore, at times when writing, I feel myself at an embodied crossroads between new wave feminism and second wave feminism. Within my writing process, I find myself justifying both feminisms and that feels comfortable. I envisage the former emphasizing 'a collective embrace of individual freedoms with broadening feminism's reach through inclusiveness and enfolded by the invisible bonds of the Internet and social media' (Shenin *et al.*, 2016). I hold on to this type of feminism, while I am aware that the latter focuses on a 'shared struggle against oppression, targeting narrowly defined enemies held together by a handful of national organizations and charismatic leaders' (Shenin et al., 2016). I have lived through this latter type of feminism during the 1970s in London, UK and for at least 15 years, it defined my ways of doing feminisms. I am aware that today's new wave feminism is more concerned with '"intersectionality" – gender, race and sexuality coming together to inform a single identity – and less concerned with women's-only spaces, in part because gender is increasingly viewed as something that is fluid, as opposed to binary' (Shenin et. al., 2016). These are all issues that I uphold and believe in strongly. Both generations of feminists 'have many questions about structural and cultural inequality and the broad spectrum of social injustice that affect diverse disempowered groups'. Second wave feminists, like myself, know that we 'will not able to find answers to these questions during our lifetime'. This is because 'new forms of inequality, injustice, human rights violations, and violence have developed that give challenges to new generation of feminists'.[4] My opinion throughout is that I am still unsure as to the feminist beliefs of my co-authors, although I thought I knew Ursula's as I was her informal mentor. But, I guess I was wrong and this knowledge makes me feel unhappy.

In '*She wrote it but look what she wrote*', in relation to my co-authors, I create a borderland space between ardour and understanding, enquiry and partiality and pure writing skill and attentive being. My own story reveals boundaries between auto (i.e. myself), ethno (i.e. the 'writing' culture, surrounding me and which, at first, my co-authors share) and graphy (i.e. the research and writing process). I embody the state of being beyond binary ('either–or') conceptions and I am forced to accept (i.e. have a tolerance for) uncertainty and paradoxes. Therefore, when my co-authors tell me that my chapters are basically not up to the mark:

> *... What we are talking about is the quality of your chapter ... our concern is that you make proclamations in your chapter that appear as unsupported and inadequately referenced – propelled by a set of postulations rather than being clearly reasoned ...'*

I believe them and am unforgivingly self-critical, asking myself, '*What went wrong?*' and not '*Am I caught in the paradox of feminist generations?*' Rather than focus on this possible, generational inconsistency, I am defensive and hurt. I wish at the time that I had asked myself, '*Why are they behaving like harsh reviewers*[5] *and not supportive, collaborators and co-authors?*' and '*Why, in my opinion, are they mirroring a masculinist political environment – taking a position connected to traditional ways of "being" in the academy?*'[6] But I did not and that also makes me unhappy. Otherwise, I would have remembered that I am outside that traditional masculinist, academic space and actively work against mirroring that type of competitive environment.

Locking on the words '*... unsupported and inadequately referenced – propelled by a set of postulations rather than being clearly reasoned ...*' confirms to me this type of mirroring and my outsider status in my co-author's eyes. I had '*... 115 references and 15 footnotes ...*' in this chapter. '*Why should I have to use the* *references they would like me to use?'*, I ask. They want me to delete my references on transgender people and ethics. I think, *'This whole experience is bizarre – they are my collaborators not academic reviewers!'* But, rather than accept the irony, I make judgements based on my emotions and this stings my body, my brain, my whole being ... *'Why not?'*, I ask myself. Rather than just outright laughing, I am secretly crying – for laughing would cut the ice, bring more understanding and perhaps enable mercy to grow between me and my co-authors – a mercy I am too afraid to embrace. *'Afterall'*, I now think, *'It's just a book not a life or death situation.'* But still at times, I find this borderland space uncomfortable and an absurdity for me. *'I am a strident feminist'*. I ponder now, *'perhaps too strident'*. I ask, *'Am I caught up in an attempt by my co-authors to practice "verbal hygiene", after all, in my opinion, I think they want to "clean up" my texts?'*

Deborah Cameron (2012: vii) contends that although 'verbal hygiene' is 'a *product* of the way language works' and is revealed in discourses and practices through which people attempt to 'clean up language and make its structure or its use conform more closely to their ideals of beauty, truth, efficiency, logic, correctness and civility ... as an impulse (it) leads to a proliferation of norms defining what is good or bad, right or wrong, acceptable or unacceptable'. Cameron also explains that those who practice verbal hygiene are regulating language and the norms they use 'may also express deeper anxieties which are not linguistic, but social, moral and political' (2012: vii). *'What are my co-authors real anxieties about my writing? Is my writing too forceful? ... Too overly political?'* I do not honestly know and am muddled, but yet my forceful beliefs and potentially overly political writing does not, in my opinion, 'hold water' for my co-authors. Perhaps, for them, my ideas are not able to be proven, not correct or not 'true'.

> *... having Betsy as first author, could give a confusing 'impression'.*

'What is that all about?' In my opinion, they want their own way, perhaps a more moderate approach, seeking their own discrete sovereignties, if not a neoliberal solution. Nevertheless, the borderlands are where I remain throughout the whole project. Although Boylorn (2014a, 2014b) demonstrates effectively how to use autoethnography to bridge racial differences, I use my autoethnography to try to bridge generational ones. This space becomes humbling and resourceful for me as I figure out how to move into different borderland spaces with a different set of feminist co-authors.[7] My feminist voice is not perfect, but at the very least it 'props me up' and gives me power and strength in my in between, bridging spaces (see Lockford, 2014). At most, it gives me sustenance in my daily life.

Autoethnography is an active demonstration of the 'personal is political'

My two stories, 'Finding my feminist voice through an illness story: an old female body confronts a thyroid problem' (Chapter 2) and *'She wrote it but look what she wrote'* (Chapter 4), reveal how misunderstandings and lack of openness, empathy[8] and trust may lead to hurt. In 'Finding my feminist voice through an illness story: an old female body confronts a thyroid problem' I ask, '*Why should a physician take seriously my (an older woman patient's) complaints and uncertainty about my ageing body?*' Giving adequate, if not appropriate, treatment implies not only making proper clinical judgements but also listening to my interpretations of what is happening to my own body. After all, the problems are embedded in my body not my doctor's. It's my body we are talking about – not hers. When diagnosing my troubling symptoms, Dr Walsh's reliance upon biomedical prejudices about menopausal women (see Caplan, 2001) is unhelpful, if not dangerous. Research (Ballard *et al.*, 2001) shows that although menopause is experienced as a status passage for older women like myself, medicalising this transition or viewing it as a pathological state (Lyons and Griffin, 2000) allows its social context to be ignored and is disempowering (Wray, 2004). Seeing me almost exclusively through the lens of menopause creates a distinctly oppressive space for my body to be blamed, managed or improved and my health to be politicised (Goldstein, 2000). Even now with developments in modern medicine, experts still do not have ways of knowing which of older women's symptoms such as palpitations, joint pains, diarrhoea, sleeplessness, numbness, dizziness and weakness are 'unavoidable concomitants of ageing' and which signify ill health (Greer, 1991: 146–8). The problem with a physician's active attribution of a deficiency disease to aging female bodies (Woods, 1999) is that bona fide diseases may be overlooked in the process, as happened to me. My problems evidenced in this story are not only physical and personal but also deeply political.

With regards '*She wrote it but look what she wrote*', my writing as a feminist scholar is, in my opinion, disparaged, and unfortunately and for my part, I feel harassed by my colleagues. During this time, I take solace from feminist friends who support me during this difficult period and encourage me to dig out of moth balls Joanna Russ's (1983) book, *How to Suppress Women's Writing* and re-read it. Of course, I take my friends' wise advice and when I start reading, I remember Russ's sensible text. Upon reflection, my writing and my experience appears to be defined as substandard, less noteworthy and less significant than my co-authors. Russ (1983: 48) argues that if women's experience is not seen, this experience will be ignored or made invisible. About women's writing she says, '"*She wrote it but look what she wrote* about" becomes "She wrote it but it is unintelligible/badly constructed/thin/spasmodic/ uninteresting, etc.", a statement by no means identical with "She wrote it but I can't understand it" (in which case the failure might be with the reader)' (1983: 48). Behind 'She wrote it, but it's unintelligible' lies the premise: 'What I don't understand doesn't exist . . .' (1983: 48). In a way, I feel as if I am socially invisible to my co-authors like so many other women authors in history. However, as Russ contends, 'The social invisibility of women's experience is not a "failure of human communication". It is a socially arranged bias persisted in long after the information about women's experience is available . . . It is . . . bad faith' (1983: 48). I am confused because my co-authors use consistently in communications with me the term, 'good faith':

> . . . they would appreciate 'in good faith' if I would leave the collaboration and sign the addendum to the contract (i.e. a contract I secured)

Sensitizing the feminist 'I' 105

> ... they want 'in good faith' to be very clear on how they want to proceed (i.e. to proceed with their own book)

> ... they 'simply want to agree the borders between their work and mine' and their email is sent 'in good faith' (i.e. the infamous 'plagiarism email').

It is difficult for me to think that any feminists would make me feel invisible, act on their socially arranged bias and evidence the sort of 'bad faith' that Russ speaks of.

The hurt I experienced in both of these stories, although obviously painful to me on a personal level, is also profoundly political, a view shared with other autoethnographers (see the Introductory chapter). But the politics of both stories differ. On the one hand, 'Finding my feminist voice through an illness story: an old female body confronts a thyroid problem' begins with me as a somewhat autonomous feminist seeking help for my debilitating illness. In the end, I find comfort and healing through collaborative personal relationships that are politically empowering. I find hope. On the other hand, '*She wrote it but look what she wrote*' begins with feminist collaboration and ends up with me being left on my own, autonomous but, in my opinion, abandoned – a collaboration gone sour and a political opportunity missed.[9] I find despair.

However, when I make a distinction between the personal and the political or even between the private and public, I need to be careful. I need to ask, '*Is this distinction a fiction?*', '*Is it real?*' or '*Is it intended to support an unjust current state of affairs?*' For example, 'our most personal acts are, in fact, continually being scripted by hegemonic social conventions and ideologies' (Felluga, 2011). Whether or not this distinction 'the personal is political' is a fiction is less important to me than how, as an emotional, embodied being I resist the status quo in the private and public entanglements in which I am involved. In short, both stories evidence this sort of resistance on my part.

Autoethnography is feminist critical writing which is performative and is committed to the future of women

In Chapter 4, '*She wrote it but look what she wrote*', I not only speak but also communicate with my writing. I am performing and making feminist action. I am consummating my feminist identity. As a feminist, I am aware that all my everyday communications are performative – even my writing. All help to define my identity. Butler (1993: xii) describes performativity as 'that reiterative power of discourse to produce the phenomena that it regulates and constrains'. Felluga (2011) contends that Butler emphasizes the ways by which identity is 'brought to life through discourse'. Performance or performativity questions 'the notion that my identity is the foundation of lesser actions such as my speech or gestures'. Butler uses her ideas on performance to clarify her radical position on gender – gender is not who we are but what we do (Felluga, 2011). Although it may be that my performative acts are enforced through the norms of society, I am what I do and I do feminism. This doing, this consummation of my feminist identity is, for my part, problematic for my co-authors as I write *Contemporary Family Issues*. Is my doing their undoing, while my undoing is their doing?

> *I am still confused as to their motivation for doing what they did. Maybe the simple reason is that I am now 'past my sell by date' so to speak ...*
>
> *... I don't know what Penelope, Ursula and Helga have been doing or said to my publishers but I have taken my publisher's advice seriously and I have not had anything more to do with them ...*

I am best situated to describe my own stories more accurately than anyone else. Through my own voice, I am able to represent myself as I live through my experiences (Wall, 2006). My performance transcends the stories I tell and signifies the everyday as text, not just to be studied but also lived and experienced (Mitra, 2010: 11). My performance centred on situational experience: how I act, what I do, how I feel, how I laugh, how others respond ... personally, in my opinion, how my co-authors make me feel, how I feel sad, hurt, confused ... autoethnography is about understanding with the other using experience, memory, emotion and performance to redefine my research objective. I am not so concerned about scientific rules and objectivity. I am wanting a sense of effervescence, embedded in my realities and framed by my resilience. My vivacity embodies me and I feel relieved that I survive.

We saw in the Introduction that Modelski (1991) talks about feminist critical writing as being 'performative' because it embodies a promise – a 'commitment to the future of women'.

In my writing, I hope to bring new meanings and new subjectivities into my reader's imagination. I have a liberatory vision. I want to contemplate; to imagine what a feminist future can be – what it will bring to our world. My fertile, feminist imagination and performance of doing something beyond restating already existent views or upholding the status quo perhaps appear problematic for my co-authors to accept.

> *We found it difficult to follow the main points of your argument. You really need to narrow down the content of the chapter ...*

Perhaps, this complex performative dimension of my writing serves to challenge their own feminist writing sensibilities. I will never know because I do not have the courage to ask. I merely feel vulnerable, hurt and in pain. All of these feelings make me weep. Did they feel triumphant or gratified?

> *They are pursuing a new contract with a new publisher and that they 'simply want to agree the borders between their work and mine – Elizabeth's ...*

Now I am Elizabeth not Betsy! I think, *'What is that formality about? Are they wanting distance from me? It makes me feel like an outcast'*. I will never know if they want distance from me, feel triumphant or gratified as I do not have the courage to ask. I reflect deeply on what happened. Along with Haraway (1994), I want to make

Sensitizing the feminist 'I' 107

a difference in the world. I cultivate Haraway's notion of diffraction.[10] I want to nurture difference, defend it and embody it. Thus, I deflect what in my opinion, I think my co-authors are doing and force my feminist ideas into my writing.

> *We feel ... sad about this, but feel it is the point to concur that we want very different things from the book.*

'*Are they sad or is this a ruse?*' I will never know as I do not have the courage to ask. With my reflexivity, I 'defuse the bombs of the established disorder' which I find in writing with my co-authors. '*Are they aware of my reflexivity or self-styled diffraction?*' I will never know as I do not have the courage to ask. This 'my not having the courage to ask' reveals a deep struggle within me and is my enormous weakness – like a debilitating curse. This becomes a prolonged, unpleasant struggle to employ my experience, memory, emotion and performance in an attempt to comprehend with my co-authors what has happened and how our writing objectives have been redefined. As my colleague George notes:

> *... the book outline talks about the authors 'demonstrating the relevance of bold concepts to practice and applying them in an overtly political way to the here and now', isn't that what you are trying to do ... I cannot see why the co-authors think that you have gone outside the parameters of the book ...*

And Deborah says,

> *Your chapter has considerable sweep and breadth, both theoretically and in terms of the empirical cases in point you bring up – but they work because you harness them to an argument for a mode of moral/empathetic interrogation (embodied ethics). I'm not sure I can see what the problem is for your colleagues.*

My 'not having the courage to ask' is an ongoing tragedy that, at times, usurps the strength of my performance. I am continually feeling bad, embarrassed and disappointed. This is an issue which my partner, Irmeli picks up:

> *You must remember that you have done nothing wrong. But, that is easy to say. I don't know whether or not you are being bullied, but if you are it is hard to deal with. You need to start feeling better about yourself.*

All of this tells me I am not perfect and neither are my co-authors.

Autoethnography helps to raise oppositional consciousness by exposing precarity

The stories, 'Being a "sexual pervert" in academia' (Chapter 1); 'Doing feminist autoethnography with drug-using women' (Chapter 3) and '*She wrote it but look what she wrote'* (Chapter 4), reveal how women on the margins, such as lesbians, drug users and retired feminists, live precarious lives.

Being 'a sexual pervert' in academia is framed by my being an out lesbian feminist sociologist in academia in the 1970s. As I said in that earlier chapter, I want to show 'how being in this situation feels'. I introduce autoethnography as a methodological tool for speaking and writing about being out in academia and how precarious this was in the 1970s, just as it can be to a certain extent today. These sentiments encapsulate my story's aim and why I feel it is important. I want to demonstrate how personal biography matters in our lives as researchers as well as how sexuality profoundly affects us – sometimes in a precarious way. Reflecting on my academic career as a member of the precariat is, as I said previously, about 'mending wounds by remembering' (Vannini, 2008: 165) and hopefully 'helping other scholars to mend their wounds'.

In 'Doing feminist autoethnography with drug-using women', I noted that the political–ideological character of autoethnographic research is explicit. I am moved emotionally by Mary's, Cheryl's, Hilary's and Jean's stories. I say that I see their lives as 'deeply human', but I also see their lives as deeply, *precariously*, human – lives worth living but at times lives lived dangerously, precariously. I want their stories and similar ones to lead readers to see that going from understanding to empathy in our work helps us to think and feel not only with our research respondents but also about ourselves and our own development as feminist researchers who, to a certain extent, share precarity with our respondents. In learning about the multiple contours of embodied drug use *vis-à-vis* their type of precarious womanhood, we should open wide the door to those autoethnographers who want to think and feel with their research stories. Outdated methodological canons that deny autoethnographers their voice and close the door to claims of authenticity need to be directly challenged. Being reflexive through autoethnography is one way of mounting this challenge and being comfortable and effective as a precarious researcher.

'*She wrote it but look what she wrote*' reveals that as feminists, we write with precarity in mind, especially those of us who are retired, old or have officially left the academy. This story exposes how, in the world of academic writing, there is an 'unequal distribution of precarity. For example, in my opinion, my co-authors' lives as 'younger' academics are seen as 'grievable and worth protecting', while my life as a retired feminist writer is viewed as 'ungrievable'. As it is, I am in the evening of my life. My life, especially my writing life is seen, is already 'lost in part' and 'less worthy of protection and sustenance'.[11] For myself, my co-authors know this and act appropriately. On the other hand, precarity reveals to me our social 'beingness' and 'our interdependency' (see Butler, 2012: 170). Although during the whole time I could challenge the normative operations of who counts in the academy, I don't. The reason why I don't is because unfortunately I do not feel a shared condition of precarity with my co-authors. This is disappointing for me because I feel that I wear a shield to protect myself from what I feel, for myself, their insults. I do not know whether or not I am rooted to a generational awareness, but I am aware acutely that my feminism is different from my co-authors.

Sensitizing the feminist 'I' 109

When analysing my story I see that perhaps a 'group think'[12] process is occurring. For example, someone in my co-authors group may be disgruntled. Perhaps it is Penelope because she wants to be lead author and is possibly envious of me; or Helga because she does not like my feminist urban work, a field she works in as well or Ursula because she is not keen on seeing herself in a mentee role any longer (*'I am grown up and do not need Betsy'*). Perhaps, Penelope and Helga come together and discuss my work critically – without my knowing – and then they engage Ursula and she joins in the discussion. Critique is whipped up as they try to impress each other on who can be most critical. Gradually, they are bonding. They are bonding in their agreement that my work is crap and their work isn't. I am wrong; they are right.

I remember the times when, in my honest opinion, my friend Ursula turned against me:

> *'Why isn't Ursula supporting me?' I ask myself. She is just silent and agrees with the others.*
>
> *I am afraid to talk out loud what I am thinking because I feel I am outnumbered and can't even depend upon Ursula any more.*
>
> *Ursula tells me, 'Do all the changes they ask, Betsy. We don't want to hold up the book. The clock is ticking'.*

In retrospect, I think, *'What clock? Is this a way to put pressure on me to cave in to their demands?'* I do not know. I only remember that in my opinion, my co-authors 'ganged up' on me in this group think process:

> *They all – my co-authors – had a chat recently. Immediately, I think, 'So I am now being excluded, totally left out – are they meeting without me?'*
>
> *We have discussed your email from 13 August (and our thoughts are below)* ...
>
> *The book has stalled because we have not been able to resolve fundamental differences between us* ...
>
> *Carol and Joe* ...
>
> *'I don't understand why am I not included in this sidebar, so to speak. Why is it not – Carol, Joe and Betsy?* ...
>
> *Carol and Joe* ...
>
> *Carol and Joe* ...
>
> ... *they* (i.e. think of their 'we') *want my assurance that I will not use any of their work as I continue with my New Publishers contract* ...
>
> ... *they* (i.e. think of their 'we') *are re-sending the email sent on 29 October* ...
>
> ... *they* (i.e. think of their 'we') *are happy to sign the addendum, in principle* ...
>
> *'We' 'We' 'We' 'We' 'We' 'We' 'We'* ...

For my part, I am being excluded in this 'group think' process. I am shaped by my own precarity as an older, retired, past my sell-by date, excluded feminist.

Although precarity is a condition of my political life, I do not feel that I share this sense, this condition with my co-authors. I want to value vulnerability and precarity without accepting social injustice and yet I don't know, but I am afraid that my co-authors may be doing an injustice not only to my writing but to my feminist character. To repeat:

> ... *they* (i.e. think of their 'we') *want my assurance that I will not use any of their work* ...

These words imply that not only am I capable of plagiarism (which, of course, theoretically I am) but also and more importantly, that given what is transpiring between my co-authors and myself, there is a real possibility, in my opinion, that I will indeed plagiarise their work. '*Why?*', I think now, '*to avenge them; to hurt them like, personally, they hurt me; to admit their work is better than my "shitty" work* ...'. I just don't know their motivation for their doing what they are doing to me and neither does my friend, Deborah:

> *I don't understand what your co-authors are trying to do, Betsy. In my opinion, I see it as really mean. Your work is always of a high standard. I don't understand their motivation. Perhaps they want the book for themselves even though the idea for the book was yours. Maybe I am being too judgmental. I don't know what to say.*

I struggle hard to foster interdependency with my co-authors. Nevertheless, in the microspaces of our political, writing lives, I embrace precarity. Although I may not feel that I share precarity with my co-authors, I inevitably do.

In her research on young women who lost their mothers, Pearce (2010: 7) shares her respondents' positions (i.e. she lost her mother at an early age) and has interesting ideas on researching vulnerability. This lengthy quote from her research is illuminating:

> Narratives cannot be separated from the context in which they were produced nor can the emotions and feelings that resulted from them ... These stories are constructions that present the 'doings' of identity, used strategically to portray one's sense of self in a certain light (Riessman, 1990, 1993) ... By being open to my own vulnerability – accepting it – allowed me to see, understand, accept the problematic narratives of others. No seamless narrative – I never really embraced this fully before – going into what it really means is quite a terrifying experience ... As Mortimore (2007: 9) describes, it felt 'as if I were dropping the researcher's protective cloak of invisibility' ... I was becoming more visible and therefore more exposed and vulnerable.
>
> (Pearce, 2010: 7)

My story, '*She wrote it but look what she wrote*' is full of emotions. Like Pearce, I am open to my own vulnerability as well as my precarity – but these two human conditions are fundamentally different. On the one hand, vulnerability, focused on the individual, is an emotional state of being in which I am open to wounding. Vulnerability can be seen as an essentialist enterprise, bounded by space and time (Ettlinger, 2007: 320). On the other hand, precarity is a 'condition of vulnerability relative to contingency and the inability to predict' – it is *collectively experienced* and renders social 'transformation conditional and difficult' (2007: 320) (emphasis added). Aware of my vulnerability, I am terrified of embracing precarity fully. More importantly, my precarity makes me frightened of my co-authors' responses which, in my opinion, are unpredictable and at times, insensitive.

As we saw earlier, precarity is 'unbounded' and in the 'evolving and intersecting governmentalities' (Ettlinger 2007: 320) of our lives, I need to refuse the separation of spheres of our feminist lives into 'older' and 'younger' generations. I need to concentrate on the relation between my own rationality and embodied emotions. I want dearly for oppositional consciousness to arise, and yet I am acutely aware that if oppositional consciousness does arise I may or may not connect with my co-authors. Although we may share precarity, I long for a cooperative politics with them – a politics based on love or, as Ensler (2015: 4) rightly says in the epigraph to this chapter, 'A love that finds value in our connection rather than in our competing'.

Autoethnography as critical feminist ethnography and the politics of going beyond structures of domination

Relying heavily upon black feminist thought and feminist standpoint theory, Sara Crawley (2012: 151), a well-established feminist autoethnographer, contends that feminist theories' greatest contribution to knowledge is an epistemological shift away from androcentric boundary-specific methods that enforce traditional binaries – rational over emotional, authoritative voices over voices of the oppressed, public over private, transcendental truths over everyday experiences – towards refusing binaries – thought as rational and emotional, multiple views and truths, everyday private and public worlds. To me this reveals the heart of the workings of feminist autoethnography. My deep need as a feminist autoethnographer is to expose my embodied, precarious subjectivity by holding myself within my skin, a skin that I am aware is white – the white of privilege – but also the tough skin of a lesbian, academic survivor.

Similar to Crawley, I see myself as a critical, feminist ethnographer. I have a dual commitment to feminist politics as well as using feminist theory as a basis for knowledge production. I have a political commitment to advance progressive social change through research and a methodological commitment to prioritize my subjects' voices (Avishai *et al.*, 2012: 395). For these researchers, this is *the* 'feminist ethnographer's dilemma'. It demands that we are reflexive *vis-à-vis* the feminisms of the institutions within which we conduct research; that as we develop our interpretive frameworks, we are cognizant of the intellectual orthodoxies they may generate and that we are mindful of how these orthodoxies relate to our research processes and the social spaces within which we conduct our research (2012: 403). Thus, in writing my autoethnography, I reflect on the feminisms of the academy and interpret carefully those hidden creative, writing and publishing spaces in which those I research (i.e. me and my co-authors, my colleagues and friends) confound these understandings. I need to live with and accept contradiction. I need both an open mind and a humble heart. I am remembering back to what I said to Penelope and Helga:

> *I like your chapters very much Penelope and Helga but I expected that your chapters would be more feminist orientated, as we agreed. I don't mean to be overly critical but ...*

Now I am thinking as I write, '*Perhaps I am too critical and should take the opportunity to allow them to respond more fully to my evaluation of their work. I should challenge them to respond. Maybe, my fear (of them thinking I am m/patronizing) closes off our conversation rather than opens it up.*' In this instance, I am desperate to hold my desperation in my skin, but it must have leaked out. Now I need to sensitise my feminist 'I' – to open up rather than close off uncomfortable connections with those around me.

Throughout this book, I have demonstrated that autoethnography is a feminist method that can be employed to sensitise the feminist 'I'. It is crucial that I am clear: my feminist 'I' is not a singular, individualistic 'I'; my 'I' is always in relation to others. The politics of my feminist 'I' begins as I am embedded in cultures that are constantly shifting, 'pluralistic, subjective, personal and potentially inclusive' (Boylorn and Orbe, 2014: 15) and embodied by my 'interpersonal experiences of gender, race, ethnicity, ability, and orientation within larger systems of power, oppression, and social privilege' (2014: 19). My politics do not begin with myself as being political; my politics arise through my embodied relations with others, relations I initiated when I invited my co-authors to write with me:

> *... I respect their work, I want to ask them if they would be interested in agreeing to co-author with me a book ... which would begin to answer some of the questions posed by my students and focus on key concepts in the field. These potential co-authors are all younger than me. I know they are solid scholars ... everyone is keen to be involved ... It is all very exciting and I am relieved that we have agreed to have a feminist thread throughout all of our writing ... 'What luck', I think, feeling contented.*

Understanding the feminist 'I' in and through autoethnography opens up the possibility of having an effect on social justice.[13] As Muncey (2010: xi) contends, 'It is the complexity of individuals' (and I would add cultures) 'that autoethnography seeks to address'.

Writing within this context of the politics of autoethnography, Norman Denzin (2014: 6) contends that autoethnographic work must 'always be interventionist', meaning that it 'gives notice to those who may otherwise not be allowed to tell their story or who are denied a voice to speak'. He contends further that autoethnography is comparable to 'écriture' feminine,[14] radical feminist discourse and critical theory' that endeavour to produce 'a radical form of writing' that contravenes structures of power – 'writing which reproduces the struggle for voice of those on the wrong side of power relationship (Denzin, 2014: 6).' This reminds me:

> Penelope says, *'There is one more issue which is about the idea of this book. It may be have been your idea but you probably agree that the way the book has developed ... was a result of mutual discussions. It has been a collaborative effort in which we have made equivalent inputs. So we agree and we hope you do too that no one person is the first author in terms of leading the authoring or thinking out of the book'.* I am thinking to myself, *'Wait a moment, I am the first author here, I invited you to be co-authors – not the other way around'.* I don't understand what is happening now.

For Denzin, this type of autoethnographic stance disturbs 'the classic oedipal logic of life history methods' which positions 'subjectivity and self-development in the patriarchal system of marriage, kinship, and sexuality' (2014: 6). For me, this stance is able to upset the hierarchical, patriarchal anticipations embedded in the academic publishing world – the masculinist perspective which, in my opinion, I believe my co-authors mirror. My autoethnographic stance activates a queer phenomenology (Ahmed, 2006).[15] Simply, my 'queer' way of thinking disturbs and rearranges my relations with my co-authors by my not following their normative or perhaps hegemonic (in terms of our book project), writing paths. Activated by their subtle reactions, my politics of disorientation place extra matters (i.e. the need to tell my story, the need for healing, the need to find my voice, etc.) within my intellectual grasp – matters that might, on the surface, appear not quite right or are uncomfortable.

In a similar, critical vein of thinking to Denzin, but speaking generally about developing an 'ethnographic attitude',[16] Haraway (1997: 22) sees ethnography as 'critical feminist technologies for producing convincing representations of the reproduction of inequality'. For Haraway, there are always risks – 'moral, political, technical and epistemological' (1997: 39). To employ Haraway's (1997: 39) 'ethnographic attitude' is all about knowing that ethnography is explicitly a method of risk. For example, although I may be at risk confronted by the processes and conversations into which I probe, I am at risk because I will confront instabilities, divergent opinions and beliefs that vary considerably from mine. Therefore, having an 'ethnographic attitude' allows me to have distinct epistemological boundaries between myself and others; to be attentive to practical and theoretical issues which arise in my research journeys and to 'remain mindful and accountable' (Haraway, 1997: 39). For me, an 'ethnographic attitude' demands an opening up to others (not a closing off or shutting down) and the social situations in which I and they participate; a clear awareness of the boundaries between mine and other's identities with an eye on 'power, oppression and privilege' and a moral and political commitment to describe what I see as honestly as possible. An 'ethnographic attitude' is also embedded in my autoethnographic work. This is because autoethnography, itself a knowledge project, remains a collective undertaking and a research practice not only involving dangers, resolves, consequences and anticipations (see Haraway, 1997: 39) but also cultivating learning practices to be at risk in the embodied, emotional work needed to tell my stories. In my autoethnographies, I may identify with those I research or I may not. Identifications may create tensions:

I feel delighted as I see this book as a way of mentoring my co-authors – they do not have much experience publishing books.

I read that they say (and remember this is my friend Ursula speaking for the others) that I have been the main contact with New Publishers, but that I have assumed no senior or mentoring role or responsibility for conceptualising the book structure or content.

I think, 'Oh dear, I initiated the project. The book was my idea. I invited them to join the project. What is happening?' I feel a knot in my stomach and again the shame wells up.

The main issue is that my identities, my pluralities of being in the world engage with the other identities, situations, emotions and embodiments of others around me. These may be unfamiliar or perhaps, anathema to me, but I need to press on. On the other hand, the risk is that I may not take up the challenge that these types of relational engagements present to me. If that is the case, my autoethnographies become inauthentic, boring, sterile and politically ineffectual – not worth writing. Critical feminist autoethnographers need to embrace these challenges in spite of what Haraway (1997) contends about risks. We need courage and steadfastness in the face of these risks. In taking up my 'ethnographic attitude' (and I would add my autoethnographic one), I am 'at risk in the face of serious non-identity that challenges previous stabilities, convictions or ways of being of many kinds' (Haraway, 1997: 37).[17] So be it. I will survive. I am willingly going beyond structures of domination and the potential risks awaiting me.

Conclusion: the way forward

In this book, my autoethnographies have transversed a variety of personal, social, economic, political and cultural contexts as I presented you stories with different configurations of multiple logics and emotions. In these stories, we saw the difficulties I had as an older woman being incorrectly treated in the NHS; how as an out lesbian I became a target of insults at my work place; how pain and empathy can be generated when doing research with drug-using women and how I was hurt when, in my opinion, my co-authors and somewhat 'younger' colleagues constructed their socially arranged bias about my writing. I tell these stories not because I wanted to show my GP as insensitive; to put the colleague who implied I was a pervert in a bad light; to make moral judgements on Hilary who was raped and not yet rehabilitated from drugs; or to condemn my co-author colleagues who, in my opinion, suppressed my writing. Rather, in each story there is a blend of logical calculations and embodied emotions that transverse personal, political, economic, social and cultural needs and rationalities. In all these stories, the personal is political. But also, the political is personal. Furthermore, I hope that exposing borderland spaces in my autoethnographies uncovers the delicate nature of using our own stories as data, as well as revealing the importance of accepting paradoxes in our contradictory lives as feminists. My performativity reveals not only my hopes for the future but also how my identity is brought to life through feminist discourse (i.e. I am what I do and I do feminism). We may or may not also see the complexities of precarity as a human condition in these stories. This is because in such layered contexts of autoethnography, precarity is a life condition, not solely negative and always already positive, allowing us to think and feel through our stories. The 'red line' or guiding idea throughout this book, *Autoethnography as Feminist Method: Sensitising the Feminist 'I'* is that autoethnography is a useful feminist method for telling our stories.

Hopefully, all four of my autoethnographic stories help us to understand the dynamics of 'personal is political' interactions; the significance of creating transitional spaces; the importance of performativity for the future of feminism and the ordinariness of conditions that give rise to precarity. Perhaps our oppositional consciousness is spurred on and raised. I genuinely hope so.

In conclusion, I continue in my autoethnographies to cultivate a visceral sense of the difference between 'a loving eye' and 'an arrogant eye', as shown in the work of the feminist philosopher Marilyn Frye who says:

> The loving eye is a contrary of the arrogant eye. The loving eye knows the independence of the other. It is the eye of the seer who knows that nature is indifferent. It is the eye of one who knows that to know the seen, one must consult something other than one's own will and interests and fears and imagination ... The loving eye is one that pays a certain sort of attention to the other ... This attention can require a discipline ... one of self-knowledge, knowledge of the scope and boundary of the self ... It knows the complexity of the other as something which will forever present new things to be known ... The loving eye seems generous to its object, though it means neither to give nor to take ... for not-being-invaded, not-being-coerced, not-being-annexed must be felt in a world such as ours as a great gift.
>
> (Frye, 1983: 75–6)

Too often, the sort of 'deviant bodies' (i.e. lesbians, drug users, sick bodies and retired feminists) that I reveal in the autoethnographies of this book are broken by 'the arrogant eye'. Autoethnography can be used as a sensitive, methodological tool for speaking about our painful, hurtful, as well as joyous experiences of being lesbians, drug users, sick bodies and old feminists. By employing the autoethnographic method, we challenge the arrogant eye, privilege the loving eye and help to create collective, intellectual, liberatory spaces within the social sciences, shaped increasingly and sadly by neoliberal landscapes. Whether as a privileged white, lesbian feminist, but still retired academic or just another LGBT (lesbian, gay, bisexual and transgender) 'deviant body', I challenge this arrogant eye and try to use the 'loving eye' in my work. I invite you to do the same. Let's be generous to those we research and employ this great gift to break down boundaries between all those 'deviant bodies' shunned by the regulatory regime of outdated raced, classed, sexual and other repressive, neoliberal practices. Let's create conversations and a sense of effervescence that transcend our traumas and cultivate the loving eye. Let's sensitize the feminist 'I'. My sincere desire in writing this book and sharing my auto-ethnographies with you is to do precisely that.

Notes

1 When I travelled on my Leverhulme visits to a number of universities, various colleagues and graduate students had differing opinions of this story. Encouraging me to write this autoethnography when we were discussing the ethics of authoethnographic writing, one graduate student at USF (University of South Florida) said that in his opinion, 'the only unethical issue in the story was the mob mentality of my co-authors conspiring against you'. He envisaged that 'writing ethically about unethical behaviour is not a problem'. Another feminist graduate student at CUNY (City University of New York) argued that in her opinion, I should 'reveal the names of my co-authors in order to warn others about their destructive behaviour', if these others were considering collaborating with them. I responded that I did not think it was necessary and did not want to damage my co-authors' reputations. Although, I was angry at the time, I said that I did not need 'to act out revenge'. I am grateful to these two graduate students for sharing their opinions with me. Furthermore, this is why it has been important all along for me to keep confidential the names of my former co-authors.
2 I am and have been using the term 'younger' sparingly in this book because I don't want to come across as being 'matronising'. These colleagues were of a different generation from me, as the reader saw in the previous chapter. However, I treated them consistently with respect as I would any person from my generation. As far as I am concerned, we are equals and age is not and has not been a dividing factor for me. But, perhaps this view was not shared with my colleagues and I came across as matronising. That is a possibility.
3 When I was writing this chapter, I read a relevant article about 'discarded journalists' (see Maharidge, 2016: 22). Maharidge is reflecting on what has happened to journalists in the US and he says, 'The tale of today's discarded journalists is, at its core, a parable of the way our economy, our whole American way of being, *sucks people dry and throws them away as their cultural and economic currency wanes.* Many older workers, not just journalists are hurting . . .' (emphasis added). When reading this article, I think, 'I know how this feels'.
4 I am grateful to Esther Chow for pointing this out in a general email sent to the Sociologists for Women in Society email list on 11 February 2016.
5 I am grateful to Carolyn Ellis for pointing this out to me.
6 I am grateful to a graduate student at USF for sharing her opinion with me on my lack of response.
7 Very soon after I reply to the review of my book proposal from New Horizons publishers, my new co-authors (including four feminists of varying ages and feminist generations) and I receive and sign a contract for *Contemporary Family Issues*. This causes me great relief.
8 In '*She wrote it but look what she wrote*', I face a dilemma: I want to take up my own positionality as well as my co-authors in this story. I want to offer them empathy. But as one graduate student at USF said, you are generous by 'giving your co-authors empathy'. 'In my opinion, I would give them hate and anger as well'. I am grateful for this interesting intervention by this student and for recognising a range of emotions in my story.
9 This tension was raised in a discussion with a graduate student at USF and I am thankful to him for our discussion.

10 See Chapter 3 for a fuller discussion of Haraway's notion of diffraction.
11 See reference to Butler (2012) in Endnote 12 in the Introduction.
12 I am grateful to Carolyn Ellis for introducing this concept of 'group think' to me and for sharing her ideas on this particular autoethnography.
13 I am grateful for Professor Margrit Shildrick for discussing this issue with me.
14 For a full discussion of 'l'écriture feminine', see Jones (1981).
15 I am grateful to Dr Kirsti Lempianen for discussing this with me.
16 I am grateful to the postgraduate students at Tema Genus – Interdisciplinary Gender Studies, Linköping University, Sweden for discussing this issue with me.
17 I am grateful to Professor Gayle Letherby who acknowledged in discussion with me the significance of recognising both 'shared or non-shared identity' in autobiographical work.

References

Ahmed, S. (2006) *Queer Phenomenology: Orientations, Objects, Others*. Durham, NC: Duke University Press.

Ahmed, S. (2014) *Willful Subjects*. Durham, NC: Duke University Press (Kindle edition).

Allen, K. R. and Piercy, F. P. (2005) 'Feminist autoethnography,' In Sprenkle, D. H. and Piercy, F. P. (eds.), *Research Methods in Family Therapy*. New York, NY: Guilford Press, pp. 155–69.

Avishai, O., Gerber, L. and Randles, J. (2012) The feminist ethnographer's dilemma: reconciling progressive research agendas with fieldwork realities. *Journal of Contemporary Ethnography* 42, 4: 394–426.

Ballard, K. D., Kuh, D. J. and Wadsworth, M. (2001) The role of menopause in women's experience of the 'change of life'. *Sociology of Health and Illness* 23, 4: 397–424.

Boylorn, R. M. (2014a) From here to there: how to use auto/ethnography to bridge difference. *International Review of Qualitative Research* (Special Issue: The Bridge Building Power of Autoethnography) 7, 3: 312–26.

Boylorn, R. M. (2014b) 'A story and stereotype: an angry and strong auto/ethnography of race, class and gender'. In Boylorn, R. M. and Orbe, M. P. (eds.), *Critical Autoethnography: Intersecting Cultural Identities in Everyday Life (Writing Lives)*. Walnut Creek, CA: Left Coast Press, pp 129–43.

Boylorn, R. M. and Orbe, M. P. (2014) 'Critical autoethnography as a method of choice'. In Boylorn, R. M. and Orbe, M. P. (eds.), *Critical Autoethnography: Intersecting Cultural Identities in Everyday Life (Writing Lives)*. Walnut Creek California: Left Coast Press, pp. 13–26.

Butler, J. (1993) *Bodies that Matter: On the Discursive Limits of 'Sex'*. New York, NY: Routledge.

Butler, J. (2012) Precarity talk: a virtual roundtable with Lauren Berlant, Judith Butler, Bojana Cvejic, Isabell Lorey, Jasbir Puar and Ana Vujanovic; edited by Jasbir Puar. *TDR: The Drama Review* 56, 4: 163–77.

Cameron, D. (2012) *Verbal Hygiene*. London: Routledge.

Caplan, P. J. (2001) Chronic fatigue syndrome: a first-person story. *Women and Therapy* 23, 1: 123–43.

Crawley, S. L. (2012) 'Autoethnography as feminist self-interview'. In Gubrium, J. F., Holstein, J. A., Marvasti, A. B. and McKinney, K. D. (eds.), *The Sage Handbook of Interview Research: The Complexity OF THE Craft*. London: Sage Publications, pp. 143–61.

Denzin, N. K. (2014) *Interpretive Autoethnography* (Qualitative Research Methods, Vol. 17). 2nd edn. London: Sage Publications.

Ellis, C. (2004) *The Ethnographic I: A Methodological Novel about Autoethnography.* Walnut Creek, CA: Altamira Press.

Ensler, E. (2015) Bureau of sex slavery. *The Nation*, 26 October, pp. 4–6.

Ettlinger, N. (2007) Precarity unbound. *Alternatives: Global, Local, Political*, 32, 3: 319–40.

Felluga, D. (2011) 'Modules on Butler: on performativity'. *Introductory Guide to Critical Theory.* 31 January, Purdue University. Available at www.purdue.edu/guidetotheory/genderandsex/modules/butlerperformativity.html (accessed 22 March 2016).

Frye, M. (1983) *The Politics of Reality: Essays in Feminist Theory.* Freedom, CA: The Crossing Press.

Goldstein, D. E. (2000) 'When ovaries retire': contrasting women's experiences with feminist and medical models of menopause. *Health* 4, 3: 309–23.

Greer, G. (1991) *The Change: Women, Ageing and the Menopause.* London: Hamish Hamilton.

Haraway, D. J. (1994) A game of cat's cradle: science studies, feminist theory, cultural studies. *Configurations* 2, 1: 59–71.

Haraway, D. J. (1997) The virtual speculum in the New World Order. *Feminist Review* 55: 22–72.

Jewkes, Y. (2011) Autoethnography and emotion as intellectual resources: doing prison research differently. *Qualitative Inquiry* 18, 1: 63–75.

Jones, A. R. (1981) Writing the body: toward an understanding of 'l'écriture feminine'. *Feminist Studies* 7, 2: 247–63.

Lockford, L. (2014) Trusting the bridging power of autoethnography. *International Review of Qualitative Research* (Special Issue: The Bridge Building Power of Autoethnography) 7, 3: 283–9.

Lyons, A. C. and Griffin, C. (2000) 'Representations of menopause and women at midlife'. In Ussher, J. M. (ed.), *Women's Health: Contemporary International Perspectives.* Leicester, UK: BPS Books, pp. 470–5.

Macdonald, J. (2013) An autoethnography of queer transmasculine femme incoherence and the ethics of trans research. *40th Anniversary of Studies in Symbolic Interaction (Studies in Symbolic Interaction)*, 40: 129–52.

Maharidge, D. (2016) Written off: veteran newspaper journalists are a dying breed. That's bad for journalism and democracy. *The Nation*, 21 March, 302, 12: 20–5.

Mitra, R. (2010) Doing ethnography, being an ethnographer: the autoethnographic research process and I. *Journal of Research Practice* 6, 1: Article M4, 1–21.

Mizzi, R. (2010) Unraveling researcher subjectivity through multivocality in autoethnography. *Journal of Research Practice*, 6, 1: Article M3, 1–14. Available at http://jrp.icaap.org/index.php/jrp/article/view/201/185 (accessed 23 March 2016).

Modelski, T. (1991) *Feminism without Women: Culture & Criticism in a 'Postfeminist' Age.* New York, NY: Routledge.

Muncey, T. (2010) *Creating Autoethnographies.* London: Sage Publications.

Pearce, C. (2010) The crises and freedoms of researching your own life. *Journal of Research Practice* 6, 1: Article M2, 1–15.

Russ, J. (1983) *How to Suppress Women's Writing.* London: Women's Press.

Shenin, D., Thompson, K., McDonald, S. N. and Clement, S. (2016) 'Betty Friedan to Beyoncé: today's generation embraces feminism on its own terms'. *Washington Post*, 27 January. Available at https://www.washingtonpost.com/national/feminism/betty-friedan-to-beyonce-todays-generation-embraces-feminism-on-its-own-terms/2016/01/27/ab480e74-8e19-11e5-ae1f-af46b7df8483_story.html (accessed 31 March 2016).

Vannini, P. (2008) A queen's drowning: material culture, drama, and the performance of a technological accident. *Symbolic Interaction* 31, 2: 155–82.

Wall, S. (2006) An autoethnography on learning about autoethnography. *International Journal of Qualitative Methods* 5, 2: 146–60.

Woods, N. F. (1999) 'Conflicting perspectives of health care providers and midlife women and consequences for health'. In Clarke, A. E. and Olesen, V. L. (eds.), *Revisioning Women, Health and Healing*. New York, NY: Routledge, pp. 343–54.

Wray, S. (2004) What constitutes agency and empowerment for women in later life? *The Sociological Review* 52, 1: 22–38.

Index

Adams, Tony 6, 11, 13, 19, 23–4, 40, 74, 98
Addiction Research Unit (ARU) 31
Ahmed, Sara 13, 19, 101, 113, 117
Allen, Katherine R. 4, 13–14, 19, 24, 42, 99, 100, 117
analytical authoethnography 18n10
Anderson, Tammy 71n5, 72
Anzaldua, Gloria 4, 19
Arendt, Hannah 19; and narrative 1, 2, 20
arrogant eye 115
art 3–4, 15–16, 20, 44, 100
autoethnography as 'artistic enterprises' 15, 100; as a 'conscious choice' 6; as 'creative nonfiction' 6; as feminist method 1, 4, 5, 6, 10, 13, 16–17, 24, 38–9, 43, 69, 99, 100, 112, 115; as 'performative' 4, 5, 9–10, 18n11, 20, 61, 71, 105–6; as political x, 2–4, 5, 6–11, 14–15, 18n6, 18n7, 18n10, 22–4, 67–8, 71 n3, 100, 103–5, 108, 110–15; core ideals of 13–17; difference with autobiography 2, 8, 18n4; ethics of 16–17, 98n1, 100–1, 116n1

de Beauvoir, Simone 30
Behar, Ruth 4, 7, 20
Bell, Susan 1, 20, 54, 57
Benhabib, Seyla 1–2, 17n1, 20
Berger, Peter 28
Berlant, Lauren 12, 20, 22, 117
Berrigan, Daniel 27
Best, Steven 54, 57
binary 3, 8, 53, 61; beyond binary 4, 102
Birkbeck College 33
black feminism 7
Bochner, Arthur xi, 2–4, 15, 18, 20–1, 44, 57–8, 60, 62, 68, 71n3, 72–3
borderland space 6, 102–3
Bourdieu, Pierre 35, 40
Boylorn, Robin 2, 7, 11, 20, 103, 112, 117

Braidotti, Rosi 6, 18n5, 20, 43, 55, 57, 83
bullied 81, 86, 100, 107; *see also* hurt; shame
Bury, Mike 54, 57
Butler, Judith 10–12, 18n11, 18n12, 20, 22, 105, 108, 117n11, 117–18

Cameron, Deborah 13, 20, 103, 117
Campbell, Nancy viii, xi, 34, 40, 70, 72
Campling, Jo 33
Carbimazole 47, 49, 50–1
Cartesian paradigm of rationality 1, 37, 54
Catholic elites 28, 42
Catonsville nine 27
Centre for Intercultural Documentation 28
Charmaz, Kathy 43, 53–4, 57
Chow, Esther 116n4
Clarke, Adele 3, 20, 43, 56n11, 57–8, 119
Connecticut xii, 25–7
consciousness raising 7, 8, 21, 32
courage, lack of 106–7
Crawley, Sara xi, 11, 14, 21, 24, 40, 111, 117
Crick, Bernard 33
critical theory 3, 39, 69, 113, 118
crying 29, 48, 67, 81, 85, 103
CUNY (City University of New York) xi, 116n1

Denzin, Norman x, 21–3, 41, 58, 61, 72–3, 112–13, 117
devastation, sense of 85, 94, 101
deviant bodies' 24, 33–4, 42, 115–16
diffraction, notion of 68, 70, 107, 117n10
Dingwall, Robert 41, 60, 72
domestic violence 63
Downes, David 29
drug users xii, 19n13, 34, 60 – 73, 108, 115

'ecriture' feminine 113, 117n14, 118
Ellis, Carolyn ix, x, xi, 2–4, 6, 9, 11, 15–16, 18n9, 19n14, 19–23, 44–5, 57–8, 60, 62, 68–9, 70n1, 72–4, 98n1, 100, 116n5, 117n12, 118
embodied – affectivity **5**, 8, 9; crossroads 4, 5, 6, 101; deviance 36–7, 42; emotionality 39
embodiment 6, 9, 11, 54–5, 57, 71n3, 78–9, 81–4, 97, 114
emotional compassing 16–17
emotional recall 16, 19n14, 45, 56n2, 60, 62, 70n1
Ensler, Eve 99, 111, 118
epistemology 14, 23; Western 13; epistemologies of ignorance 34, 40n6, 42
essentialist viewpoint 53
ethically accountable 16–17, 62, 98n1
ethnographic attitude 99, 113–14
Ettlinger, Nancy 12–13, 21, 111, 118
Ettorre, Elizabeth 3, 11, 21, 30–5, 40n8, 40–1, 61, 70, 71n3, 72–3
European Commission 35
excluded 37, 84, 109–10; excluded feminist 110
Exley, Sonia 45, 58

Facebook 8
faith (bad) 104–5; faith (in good) 85, 91, 94, 104–5
FBI 27
Felluga, Dino 105, 118
feminism (radical) 31, 113
feminist autoethnographer 4, 5, 14, 16, 60, 71n4, 74, 100, 111, 114
feminist autoethnography 4, 5, 13, 15, 17, 18n8, 19, 21, 37, 43, 67, 99–100, 107–8, 111, 117; as feminist method 4, 13
feminist fieldwork 1, 14, 22
feminist generations 101–2, 116n7; new generation of feminists 8; Second wave feminists 6, 18n6, 79, 88, 101–2
feminist 'I' ix, 17, 39, 56, 74, 98–9, 112, 115–16
feminist method ix, xi, 1, 4, 5, 6, 10, 13, 16–17, 22, 24, 39, 43, 69, 99–100, 112, 115
feminist sociology 24, 29, 37
feminist theory 9, 10, 12, 22, 57, 73, 111, 118
Fitzpatrick, Father Joe 27
Fordham University 27, 29
Foucault, Michel 36, 41, 43, 54, 58
Frank, Arthur 43–4, 54–5, 58, 70, 73
Freire, Paulo 28
Frye, Marilyn 115, 118

Gagnon, John 29
generational inconsistency 102
genetics 24, 35–6, 40n7, 41
Glassner, Barry 22, 24, 41
Glazer, Daniel 29
Greer, Germaine 30, 104, 118
grievable (and worth protecting) 19n12, 108; *see also* ungrievable
grounded theory 3, 20, 57
group think 109–10, 117n12

Hanisch, Carol 8, 21
Hanmer, Jalna 30, 42
harassed (I feel) 80–1, 92, 104
Haraway, Donna 67–9, 73, 106–7, 113–14, 117n10, 118
Hartnoll, Richard 33
Harvard University 28
Heapy, Brian 67, 73
Helsinki i, viii, xii, 34, 38, 46, 76–9, 84–5
herbal medication 49, 50–1, 54–5
heroin 34, 63–4, 71n10
Hertz, Rosanna xii, 22, 24, 41
Hesed 17, 19n17
Hirst, Paul 33
HIV 33
Holland, Janet 33
Holman-Jones, Stacy ix, x, 6, 9, 11, 14, 19, 22–4, 40, 98
hooks, bell 9–10, 21
hope 6–7, 10, 12, 29, 31, 74, 97, 100, 105, 115
Human Genome Project 35
hurt 7, 17, 19n16, 27, 32, 34, 78, 87, 100, 102, 104–6, 110, 114–15, 116n3; *see also* bullied; shame

identity 1, 29, 30, 32, 35, 43, 45, 52, 54–6, 56n12, 70, 83, 102, 105, 110, 114–15, 117n17; infirmity identities 54–5
Illich, Ivan 28
insults 31, 108, 114; *see also* shame
interdependency 12, 108, 110
intersectionality 102
irony 95, 103

Kellner, Douglas 54, 57
Kleinman, Sherryl 1, 14, 22
Krieger, Susan 24, 41

la mestiza 4
laughing 58, 81, 103
lesbian battering 7

Index

lesbians 24, 29–31, 34, 41–2, 60, 108, 115
Letherby, Gayle xi, 45, 58, 117n17
Leverhulme Trust ix, x, xi, 2, 38, 90, 92, 116n1
LGBTQI 8, 24, 35–6
libel 93–5, 98n4; *see also* plagiarism; reputation
Lipow, Arthur 33
London, England xi, 24, 29–30, 32, 38, 40n3, 64–5, 102
London School of Economics 24
Lorde, Audrey 60, 70, 73
Lorey, Isabell 11, 20, 22, 117
loving eye 115–16

Macdonald, Joe 24, 41, 101, 118
MacGregor, Susanne viii, xi, xii, 33, 41
Maharidge, Dale 116n3, 118
Mamo, Laura 83
Martin, Emily 53–4, 58
masculinist perspective 113
mending wounds (by remembering) 108
menopause 43, 46, 52–3, 58, 104, 117–18
mentor, mentoring 75–7, 85, 89, 101–2, 114
Modelski, Tania 9–10, 22, 106, 118
'modernist observers' 61
Morris, Terence 30, 42
'mulitvocality' 101, 118
Muncey, Tessa 112, 118

narrative 1–3, 7, 15–16, 17n1, 18n4, 19n14, 19n15, 20–3, 42, 45, 53–4, 57–8, 60–2, 67–8, 70, 71n3, 72–3, 101, 110; parallel narratives 68–9, 70
neoliberal 10; solution 103
News of the World 32
NHS 46, 48–50, 56n4, 56n9, 114
nomadic flexibility 43, 52–3, 55

oedipal logic of life history methods 113
Olesen, Virginia 43, 56n11, 57, 119
oppositional consciousness 4, 5, 11, 13, 107, 111, 115
oppressive space 104
Orbe, Mark P. 112, 117

Parsons, Talcott 28
Perrone, Dina 60, 70n1, 73
Piercy, Fred 4, 13–14, 19, 99–100, 117
Pimlott, Ben 33
pipsqueaks 87–8, 93
plagiarism 91–2, 94–5, 105, 110; *see also* libel
Plummer, Ken xi, 24, 40n3, 42
polyvocality 101

postmodern 3, 8, 39, 57, 61, 73–4; postmodern turn 20, 61, 70; postmodernist witnesses 61, 71n3, 71n4
precarity 4–5, 11–13, 18n12, 20, 22, 68, 107–8, 110–11, 115, 117; precarity as unbounded 21, 111, 118

queer phenomenology 13, 19, 113, 117; 'queer' way of thinking 113

Reed-Danahay, Deborah 2, 3, 22
reflective research, four elements in 67
reflexivity xii, 14–15, 19, 21, 40, 58, 61, 68–9, 70, 73, 107; self-reflexivity 16, 19n13, 100
Reinharz, Shulamit 6, 22
reliability 44, 61, 68–9
Rensselaer Polytechnic Institute xi, 17n2
reputation 28, 30, 92–4, 98n4, 116n1; *see also* libel
retired ix, 39, 77–8, 100–1, 108, 110, 115
Richardson, Laura 15, 22, 70, 73
Riska, Elianne viii, 34, 41
Rock, Paul 29
Rose, Hilary 30, 42
Roth, Julius 43, 58
Rothman, Barbara Katz xi, xii, 2, 22
Rupp, Leila 84
Russ, Joanna 104–5, 118

Sarachild, Kathie 7, 23
science 3, 15, 36, 42, 44, 73, 100, 118
self 1–3, 5, 7, 16, 17n1, 18n3, 19n14, 22, 36, 41, 43, 45, 52–5, 57, 58, 61; vulnerable self 3–4, 68, 71n3, 83, 110, 115; writing the self ix, xi, 2, 38–9
shame 49, 80–2, 84, 87–90, 94, 97, 114; *see also* bullied; hurt
Sisters of Mercy 25, 27
Skype 75–9, 80–1, 89–90, 92, 95
Smart, Carol xi, 2, 23–4, 33, 42, 75
Socialist Workers Party 30
social justice 11, 28, 112
sociology ix, xi, 3, 27–31, 35–6; of the body 24, 35, 37, 83; feminist 24, 29, 37; medical 44, 54, 61, 71n3
solicitor 91–3, 95
Soothill, Keith 30
Sparkes, Andrew 3, 23, 69–70, 72n26, 73
Stacey, Judith 6, 23
Stanley, Liz 2, 18n3, 23

Index   123

Steinberg, Deborah Lynne xii, 36, 40n7, 42
Students for a Democratic Society (SDS) 27
substance use viii, xii, 33–4, 41, 73

Taylor, Verta 32, 42, 84
Terry, Jennifer 36, 42
Thryrotoxicosis 43, 46
Tuana, Nancy 40n6, 42
Turner, Bryan 43, 54, 58

ungrievable 19n12, 108; *see also* grievable
University of Liverpool i, viii, xii, 40n5
University of Plymouth i, xi, 35
University of South Florida xi, 116n1

untrustworthy 87, 90–1
Urla, Jacqueline 36, 42

validity 61, 69, 100
Vannini, Phillip 11, 23–4, 42, 108, 119
verbal hygiene 103, 117
verisimilitude 45, 69, 100
vulnerability 1, 5, 7, 11–12, 99, 110–11

Walker, Alice 43, 56, 58
wilful 55, 101
Women's liberation 5, 8, 9, 10, 21, 30, 32, 42; Movement 7

Zabida, Sami 33
Zola, Irving 43, 59

Taylor & Francis eBooks

Helping you to choose the right eBooks for your Library

Add Routledge titles to your library's digital collection today. Taylor and Francis ebooks contains over 50,000 titles in the Humanities, Social Sciences, Behavioural Sciences, Built Environment and Law.

Choose from a range of subject packages or create your own!

Benefits for you
- Free MARC records
- COUNTER-compliant usage statistics
- Flexible purchase and pricing options
- All titles DRM-free.

REQUEST YOUR FREE INSTITUTIONAL TRIAL TODAY

Free Trials Available
We offer free trials to qualifying academic, corporate and government customers.

Benefits for your user
- Off-site, anytime access via Athens or referring URL
- Print or copy pages or chapters
- Full content search
- Bookmark, highlight and annotate text
- Access to thousands of pages of quality research at the click of a button.

eCollections – Choose from over 30 subject eCollections, including:

Archaeology	Language Learning
Architecture	Law
Asian Studies	Literature
Business & Management	Media & Communication
Classical Studies	Middle East Studies
Construction	Music
Creative & Media Arts	Philosophy
Criminology & Criminal Justice	Planning
Economics	Politics
Education	Psychology & Mental Health
Energy	Religion
Engineering	Security
English Language & Linguistics	Social Work
Environment & Sustainability	Sociology
Geography	Sport
Health Studies	Theatre & Performance
History	Tourism, Hospitality & Events

For more information, pricing enquiries or to order a free trial, please contact your local sales team:
www.tandfebooks.com/page/sales

Routledge
Taylor & Francis Group

The home of Routledge books

www.tandfebooks.com

Printed in Great Britain
by Amazon